LEADING
WITH
IMPACT

Keith Bleasdale

This book is dedicated to those leaders who are committed to making the workplace a better place.

Leadership is a huge topic, and a single book cannot come close to covering every aspect. There are many excellent books available that focus upon the academic perspective and, similarly, many that focus on the development of specific leadership skills. This book aims to bridge the gap, to provide a reference source that is academically robust and also practical and useable.

The content is based upon my own experience of having led teams, from having studied the subject at an advanced level, and from the privilege of working with and supporting literally thousands of practising leaders.

I hope you find the content interesting, insightful and accessible, and that it contributes towards your understanding of leadership, encourages you towards greater self-awareness, and offers some insights into how to upgrade the way you lead.

The end result is that you fulfil your responsibility as a leader to help you bring out the best in others; that way, *everybody* wins.

First published in 2018

Published by One Point One Ltd

Copyright © Keith Bleasdale 2018

Design, illustrations and editorial by Ben Bleasdale

Acknowledgements

To my soulmate Astri, and my pride and joy Dan & Ben

Huge Thanks

First, to you Ben, for all your research, creativity and painstaking work on the design and graphics of the book. Producing the book jointly with you made it possible, and made it a pleasure too.

Second, to (in alphabetical order) Adrian Powell, Astri Bleasdale, Joe Wheeler, John Bleasdale, Mark Nugent, Peter Brown, and Sally Howard for giving so much of their time and insights to review draft versions. You helped me iron out the rough spots and make countless improvements.

Third, to the countless people who have supported my learning throughout life, including all of the professionals within the leadership field whose insights have taught me so much; I have tried faithfully to credit you wherever I could.

The six sections of the book address key aspects of leadership:

Section I: The Role of Leadership

Leadership has evolved through four notable themes, becoming ever-more complex and transparent, and today's leaders require a broader range of skills and are exposed to far greater scrutiny than ever before. Through all of these demands, leaders remain accountable for creating great inclusive workplaces, and demonstrating integrity and consistency in the process.

Section II: The Leader's Outlook

This section looks at some of the key 'mindsets' that underpin great leadership. For all of us, our outlook on life determines so many things, and that impact is magnified in the case of leaders because of their influence over others.

Section III: Key Leadership Skills

Ultimately, the only way we can judge another person is by what they have said and done, in other words by their behaviours. So, leaders must *do* the right things, and this section looks at key skills areas that they must demonstrate.

Section IV: The Mark of a Leader

Good leaders share certain characteristics in the way they operate and the qualities they bring to their leadership roles, which set them apart. They enable those who aspire to lead to cope with the demands of their role, and result in them being admired and positive role models.

Section V: Key Points

A brief summary of key points from each chapter.

Section VI: The Future of Leadership

Our world is changing faster than ever, and leadership is already adapting to our more fragmented, diverse, transparent and unpredictable workplaces. This section takes a snapshot view of key changes that are emerging, and how leadership might change in response, evolving perhaps into a 'fifth theme'.

Contents

Introduction

I have often wondered why so many authors start their books by explaining why they embarked on the task. Now that it's my turn I finally appreciate it's the opportunity to flag what the book hopes to achieve, and how it might do that. For me the rationale is simple; it is the massive impact that leadership has on performance. And by 'performance' I don't just mean 'output'; I mean also the ability to attract and retain talent, create workplaces that people enjoy, promote positive behaviours in others, help people achieve their potential, build positive relationships and ultimately enjoy their work.

As if these factors weren't reason enough to focus on good everyday leadership, we have a weight of evidence crashing down upon us, reinforcing how all these things impact so significantly upon people's health and wellbeing. Great leadership really is a virtuous circle, and practising good leadership costs nothing. In fact, it's poor leadership that costs. So whether you consider high performance to be an aspiration for success, an imperative for survival, or simply 'the right thing to do', the days of treating good leadership as a 'nice to have' are long gone.

For almost two decades I have had the pleasure of working with practising leaders across all levels of organisations, and so the emphasis within *Leadership for Today* is upon the practical aspects that define the real job of a leader, those everyday interactions and behaviours that make the difference. Reflecting this, and also the 'busy-ness' of today's life, the layout and structure of the book is designed to be straightforward and easy to dip in and out of.

I've done everything I can to reference the book's content, but forgive me for any lapses. It's been a long journey, and sometimes you are left remembering the insight but not the source. So to all those who've been a part of my leadership journey I express my thanks for your support, friendship, and the ideas and experiences you've shared along the way. In themselves they are all great examples of leadership, and I hope my curiosity always matched your insight.

Leadership: *"Advanced Simplicity"*

Despite bookshelves straining under the weight of academic research and leadership publications, anecdotal evidence suggests that most people regularly experience instances of poor leadership, and sadly rather less frequently report that they are fortunate to work with excellent leaders. Why this should be, when excellent leadership is something we instinctively recognise and could adopt quite easily, is worth considering.

In many respects leadership is *simple,* because successful leaders have just three fundamental responsibilities; they must **engage, enthuse** and **enable** people.

In other words, they build a track record and reputation that make them appealing to others; they attract people's attention and they *engage* them. Once they have that engagement they *enthuse* others, motivating by their words and even more so by their actions. Finally, they do whatever is necessary to *enable* others to achieve their goals. The mindset of the best leaders is less about their own agenda or status, and more about their responsibility to support others' performance. You *have* to be oriented towards others, not towards yourself, and too many people stumble at that first hurdle.

This is why the best leaders have the integrity to self-reflect. After all, being able to lead yourself is a pre-requisite to being able to lead others, and there are some key questions that aspiring leaders must consider. For example, *"If my team could choose their leader, would they choose me?"* (Engage), *"Do people smile when I walk into the room ... or when I walk out of the room?"* (Enthuse), and *"Do my team feel more productive when I'm away?"* (Enable). Those questions may sound obvious and even mischievous, but in reality the answers are not always what leaders hope to hear. In other words, despite their lofty title, senior status, technical expertise, etc. the reality is they are not recognized as anything beyond their hierarchical position as 'the boss'. That said, the best leaders don't confuse 'leadership' with 'friendship'; those two are not always compatible, because at times a leader needs to confront difficult issues and make unpopular decisions. However, whilst the goal is not to become a 'friend', it is invariably helpful to be a 'friendly leader'. The whole problem might surface with one very direct question: *"Do you like working with me?"* Now, asking that takes courage!

Yet, whilst understanding leadership is simple, it is *practising* good leadership that is *'Advanced'*. This may in part be due to occasional complex strategic and inter-personal aspects, but far more frequently so because leadership is so intensely personal. There isn't an elusive formula that ensures success; just think about the wide range of styles adopted by leaders you've admired, who all operated in their own unique way. Personal authenticity is essential, so the task of developing leaders includes helping individuals build their own style and capability; we might call it their 'brand'. Good leaders need to really understand the changing face of leadership, they need to understand themselves and others, and they need to possess core leadership skills. Leadership may be *simple,* but its application is *advanced*. It's a fascinating personal development journey, and the prize is outstanding performance.

Section 1:
The Role of Leadership

Chapters:

1. Leadership is Changing

2. Creating a Great Workplace

3. Values-based Leadership

Leadership is Changing 1

Like all human endeavours, leadership evolves, and today's leaders need a much broader range of skills, and are held to account with far more transparency than in previous generations. There is broad agreement amongst researchers that the evolution of leadership has moved through four identifiable themes: *Domination, Negotiation, Inspiration* and *Inclusion*.

The themes have not replaced each other; rather each has built upon the former to create a multi-layered approach to leadership. That is worth re-stating; the best leaders are capable of adopting each of the four styles, and know when each is most appropriate. Think of it as a 'leadership toolkit', and just as when all you have is a hammer then everything looks like a nail, leaders who have only one way to lead can only ever have intermittent success.

Let's take a look at the themes and how they have emerged:

1. Domination:

In his book *Revolution: The History of England (Vol IV)*, Peter Ackroyd paints a gloomy picture of the dreadful working conditions that typified the early industrial era. As we 'progressed' through the 18th Century, increasingly workers moved from farms to factories, where they met factory owners able to capitalise fully on people's poverty, with desperate workers queueing for gruelling work at pitiful wages. England was 'a culture in which someone could be bought and sold as easily as a piece of plate', and workers had zero rights. Daniel Defoe, trader and author (most famously for his novel *Robinson Crusoe*), argued how unnecessary it was for children to be destitute, extolling the virtues of the factories: "The very children after four or five years of age, could every one earn their own bread." Workers describe how children aged as young as seven "had to rise at five every morning ... and submit to the cane whenever convenient to the master." Children who misbehaved were shackled to their machines, many suffering malnutrition, chronic fatigue, depression and deformation of muscles and bones.

It was a harsh existence for the working classes, and songwriter Joseph Mather, born in Sheffield in 1737, lamented in one of his songs that he had been born into a beggar's life from which there was no escape from creditors, bailiffs and servitude. One of his songs concludes depressingly with the line: "Which makes me curse my station, and wish I'd never been born." They were bleak times indeed, and the treatment of the working class in that era provides the starkest validation of the saying, "Power corrupts, and absolute power corrupts absolutely."

But absolute power, such as that a monarch might wield, always faces the prospect of attack. The English philosopher John Locke argued that to govern legitimately, authorities must have the consent of the governed. And whilst it is always difficult and dangerous to overthrow an absolute authority, history is littered with examples of precisely that happening, such as the overthrowing of the power-wielding English king James II in favour of the more moderate William III, or the American and French revolutions of the late 18th Century. True to Locke's philosophy, there is much historical evidence to support his view that to rule successfully, even those with seemingly absolute power must attend to the 'general will' of the people.

As the Industrial Era progressed into the 20th Century, workers' rights began to be taken more seriously, predominantly through the formation of Unions. As a result, the extremities of workplace domination eased. However, 'strong power' remained prominent in most workplaces. The prevailing view of leadership at that time was based upon the 'great man' theory, which proposed that certain people or, more accurately, certain *classes* of people, were 'born leaders'. And, big surprise, they pretty much all were male, came from the privileged upper-class, and went to the 'right' school. It would be naïve to think we have eliminated these inherent advantages however, as we will see later in this chapter, meritocracy is strongly on the rise.

I'm not disputing that some people have the good fortune to be blessed with more than their fair share of innate traits.

Take Charles Burgess Fry for example, surely the greatest all-rounder in British sport. Best known as a cricketer, he scored 2 centuries for England, captaining the team 6 times, and 92 centuries for his county team. He was also an outstanding athlete (holding the world record for the long jump for 21 years), played soccer for England, and rugby for the Barbarians. He once scored 100 runs for Sussex just two days after playing in the FA Cup final. Off the field, Fry was no slouch either; he wrote a novel and an autobiography, launched a magazine, stood for Parliament and most bizarrely was offered the throne of Albania, because representatives of that country so admired his statesman-like demeanor!

Fry, clearly, was no ordinary man, but let's be very clear that you don't *have* to be born with superpowers to be a leader, and you also don't need to be perfect; the famous cricket commentator John Arlott commenting: *"Charles Fry could be autocratic, angry and self-willed: he was also magnanimous, extravagant, generous, elegant, brilliant, and fun ..."* concluding: *"... he was probably the most variously gifted Englishman of any age."*

Despite his 'gifts', Fry was a determined character and hugely committed to whatever he set out to achieve. And so leadership is for everyone who has the will; we all can develop our leadership capabilities in precisely the same way as we develop our sporting skills, or academic skills, or sales skills, or parenting skills or any skills you can think of. You do it by raising your understanding of what it takes to succeed as a leader, by taking an honest look at yourself and then setting about developing the qualities and skills that you need. In short, we are all of us 'born leaders', *everyone* having the capacity to lead. Never make DNA an excuse.

Regardless of this exciting potential within all of us, the era of 'domination' was rarely about bringing out the best in others. Instead it was about teaching and enforcing obedience, ensuring work was undertaken in a clearly prescribed way. The role of supervisors was to ensure everyone adhered to these rigid systems, and anyone stepping outside of the rule book would be labelled a troublemaker. Business expressions such as "It's my way, or the highway" epitomise those business leaders who still choose to wield absolute power. For them, leadership is *all* about authority, yet what is beyond dispute today is that if you truly want the best out of people you have to connect with them, involve them in a respectful way, and ensure they feel connected to the success of the business.

But before we totally discount the theme of *domination*, let's recognise that it most definitely is not *all* bad, and that it does not have to be dispensed in a bullying style. When consistency is a critical success factor, then clarity and conformity become key, and thus a dominating, or we might call it 'directive', style of leadership has an important place. You would expect to encounter this style, very appropriately, in disaster and emergency situations, where there is minimal time available for consultation and conversation. In more normal scenarios, take for example the airline industry, and notably the role of the flight crews who operate in an extremely regulated environment; they do what they do in a precisely prescribed way and their routines are non-negotiable, and we are all safer as a result. If leaders had a toolkit, they would need a tool that delivered clarity and direction, through a no-nonsense directive style of leadership.

Before we move on from the theme of Domination, let's take a step back to the teachings of the ancient Greeks, to see if there is a fit. It was Aristotle who proposed there were five ways to rule a society:

1. The rule of *monarchy* referring to 'rule by one' in the interests of many.

2. The rule of *tyranny*, again the 'rule of one' but in the sole interest of the tyrant.

3. The rule of *aristocracy*, literally 'rule by the best' in the interests of many. Interestingly, Aristotle considered character and ethics to be the central criteria in defining 'best'. In today's world, the central criteria are more probably skills and output, and we would instead use the term *'meritocracy'*.

4. The rule of *oligarchy*, meaning 'rule by a few' invariably based upon wealth, ruling in their own self-interest.

5. The rule of *democracy*, meaning 'rule by the people' in the interests of the many.

If we apply Aristotle's concepts to the business world, it is easy to find parallels for each, and in doing so we can critique how and why each has potential strengths and weaknesses.

In terms of workplace leadership, 'tyranny' and 'oligarchy' most obviously align to the leadership theme of Domination. Even tyrants can succeed in business if they have the ability to control people without completely undermining their ability to perform, together with a good supply of desperate job applicants willing to replace the inevitable casualties. In addition, such leaders will need single-handedly to have all the ideas necessary for running their business, and at a personal level they must be devoid of the need for genuine human warmth and interaction. In a similar but generally less oppressive way, oligarchs command power that is almost absolute. Employees have no real choice but to dance to the oligarchs' tune; it is the oligarchs who 'pay the piper', and they who 'call the tune'. In return, workers receive the minimum rewards required to sustain the system, and the few in power retain the rest.

Action Point:

Take a step back and consider whether you might at times wear your badge of office too conspicuously. When the pressure's on, do you resort too quickly to a 'Tell' style of leadership?

Do you ask, or demand of others, to do things you wouldn't be prepared to do? If so, reflect whether that is reasonable and justified?

When you reflect honestly, are you guilty sometimes of over-looking others' ideas and contributions, whilst busily issuing directives about what *you* think should happen?

How often do you find yourself saying things like: "I'm not sure how we can do this", "Does anyone have any ideas about ...?", or "Would you give it a try and let me know how it goes." If your answer is: "Not very often", then you need to get out of the *domination* rut.

2. Negotiation:

In most mainstream businesses the leadership theme of *Negotiation* came to the fore during the 1980's, when organisations began to implement management systems such as Managing by Objectives (MBO) and Performance Related Pay (PRP). Often referred to as 'transactional' leadership, the *negotiation* theme rested on the manager and subordinate striking a deal: "If you deliver 'x', we'll reward you with 'y'." In most cases, 'y' equalled money, car, promotion, status, office, keys to the executive washroom and other such trappings of success typically referred to as 'extrinsic motivators'. This shift towards a *meritocracy*, where the best performers received the rewards and career advancement that more fairly matched their output, had to be welcome news for those who aspired to do well and worked hardest to achieve that. Also, in doing so, it struck a blow to nepotism, triggering a shift away from 'rule by the elite' and those with the right personal connections, and towards the literal meaning of Aristotle's *aristocracy*, 'rule by the best'.

In theory, at least, it is a flawless system, and yet barely more than a decade had passed before authors and researchers began to challenge the viability of relying exclusively on this type of 'deal'. Charles Handy, management guru and author of *The Hungry Spirit* wrote: "It is clear that the psychological contract between employers and employed has changed. The smart jargon now talks of guaranteeing 'employability' not 'employment' which, being interpreted, means "don't count on us, count on yourself!" Similarly, Naomi Klein observed in *No Logo* that: "A sense of impermanence is blowing through the labour force" as organisations find "ways to cut ties with their workforce." "One thing is certain," Klein observes, "offering employment – the steady kind, with benefits, holiday pay, a measure of security ... has fallen out of economic fashion." But there is a predictable cost of reducing commitment and loyalty to employees, because 'behaviour breeds behaviour', and it soon becomes a two-way street.

Loyalty (if you can call it that) to organisations, now extends only to the point where employees cannot get a better deal elsewhere. If they can, why on earth would they stay? I came across research recently from a major organisation that revealed the 'younger generation' will have 10 jobs - by the time they are 38. I can't speak for the precise accuracy of the data, but if it is even close to the truth then surely such short-termism, and therefore such lack of 'skin in the game', represents an ineffective and unappealing 'Lose:Lose' employment scenario. When you consider also the financial pressure of providing ever-increasing extrinsic motivators, then the limitations of the *Negotiation* leadership style are clear.

Then we must consider the practical challenges of implementing this reward system in a fair and effective way. The jury is out for most people when it comes to Performance Management (PM) systems. Yet there has to be a place for the *negotiation* style, and the evidence is that the vast majority of organisations globally continue to choose to retain a PM process, with only a tiny percentage reporting that they plan to remove such systems. It is no surprise, because few can argue that it makes perfect sense to establish clarity around what is expected of an employee, what support will be made available by the business, and what will be the rewards of achieving, or consequences of failing.

Supporting that, the Journal of Personality and Social Psychology reported that motivation to improve productivity increases by nearly 60% when there is a challenging goal and feedback is given on progress. Similarly, Gallup's 2017 'State of the American Workplace' survey evidences that the 21% of respondents who 'strongly agree' that their performance is managed in a motivating way, including regular development conversations and feedback with their manager, are 3 times more likely to be 'engaged'. It's completely intuitive that setting goals, giving feedback, and rewarding people appropriately are essential components of good leadership.

Despite this, survey ratings for 'employee satisfaction with PM processes' are notoriously poor, even in companies that are recognised as high performing. The criticism is not just about 'how it feels to be performance managed', but also 'whether it leads to a fairer reward system' and even more fundamentally 'whether it actually has any positive impact on results'. Why is it then that PM systems so often are disliked and criticised? What seems clear is that for many organisations their objective process of managing performance has become over-engineered and time-intensive, and with features like 'forced ranking' along a predetermined distribution curve, it is seen by many as a blunt and dehumanising tool. No one in their right mind would force-rank their family or friends, so we cannot be surprised at its lack of popularity in the workplace, and the divisiveness it can at times cause.

In recent years we have seen high-profile organisations such as Deloittes, Accenture and Microsoft start to remove forced ranking, and pare back on major parts of their PM systems. At the same time, management research firm CEB reported that nearly 90% of HR leaders believe their PM processes don't even yield accurate information, going on to state: "Employees that do best in PM systems tend to be the employees that are the most narcissistic and self-promoting." Perhaps that is not all bad, but you have to be cautious if that is the effect of your PM system.

PM systems are also challenged by the limitations of measurement systems generally. How, for example, can they measure loyalty, consideration for colleagues, attitude towards development, acting with discretion, showing kindness, or how well someone represents your department or organisations etc.? There are so many components to a person's overall contribution that are incredibly difficult to quantify. As Management guru Peter Drucker put it: *"Management by objectives works if you know the objectives. Ninety percent of the time you don't."* If, for example, Emotional Intelligence author Daniel Goleman is right in estimating that our 'IQ' accounts for around $1/3^{rd}$ of our success, whilst our emotional intelligence, our 'EQ', accounts for $2/3^{rd}$, then the limitations of a rigid objective-centric PM system become clear.

Intelligent organisations have responded to this problem by measuring not just the tangible outputs expected i.e. the *what's*, but also the way in which people behave i.e. the *how's*. This has been a welcome extension to the PM processes, and entirely appropriate as the concept of EQ shows. Yet it brings with it a huge challenge in terms of how accurately and fairly that more subjective component of performance can be isolated, observed and rated. If, for example, you tell me that my rating will incorporate how well I contribute to the team, and you then give me a huge workload that demands I work with my head down all day to deliver that, am I then penalised for not contributing to the team?

"Many of the things you can count, don't count. Many of the things you can't count, really count." Einstein

Additionally, a common limitation within recruitment is the widely-accepted notion that people are innately inclined to 'recruit in their own likeness', which is hardly surprising. It follows, therefore, that the goal of an assessee becomes to mimic the behaviours that their particular assessor most values. Whilst organisations encourage consistency by clarifying their desired Values and behaviours, we all know full-well that behaviours ultimately boil down to individual interpretation and preference. If you as team leader are highly gregarious, and consider a 'good team player' to be someone who is highly social and integrated, would you then undervalue colleagues who have a quieter style, even though they may well equally look out for opportunities to support the team and are quietly considerate at all times?

In summary, the theme of *negotiation* undoubtedly made great contributions to the field of leadership, in terms of offering clarity and implementing a far greater sense of meritocracy, and that has to be applauded. However, for many, the processes can feel rigid and unwieldly, and being exclusively 'transactional' discourages loyalty and fondness for an organization. Add to that the huge challenge of properly incorporating the critical 'softer' contributions that people make, which so often are 'the difference that makes the difference', and the limitations of the *negotiating* style become clear.

To be clear, let's not 'throw the baby out with the bathwater'; PM systems can be highly effective, and they have helped enormously in moving organisations away from basing rewards upon things like 'time served' and 'how much your boss likes you'. But the old acronym, KISS, meaning 'Keep It Simple, Stupid' has emerged as critical in the implementation of PM. Reflecting this, let's leave the final word to Accenture CEO, Pierre Nanterme: *"The art of leadership is not to spend your time measuring, evaluating ... It's all about selecting the person. And if you believe you selected the right person, then you give that person the freedom, the authority, the delegation to innovate and to lead with some very simple measure."*

🔆 Action Point:

It is a good leader's responsibility to use the PM system constructively, not to be constrained by forms and to set goals relevant to the business and the individual, to manage people differently and appropriately, and to provide honest and pertinent feedback. Take some honest soundings from colleagues regarding how they feel about how *you* operate your PM system. Find out which elements they find performance-enhancing and motivational, and which have the opposite effect. The final decision is yours of course, but you should at least know what colleagues think and reflect upon any improvements that you might make.

3. Inspiration:

The word inspiration derives from the Latin *'spiro'*, which means 'to breathe life into'. Thus, inspirational leaders spark an energy in those around them; in simple terms they put a spring in their step. They make work a positive experience, sometimes even a pleasure. So, how do they do that? Well, it is primarily about helping people embrace the *purpose* of their job, i.e. helping them to see *why* they do what they do, and then taking the time and trouble to recognize and praise people for doing so.

Imagine a hotel receptionist working alongside a hotel manager whose style is a combination of Domination and Negotiation. The receptionist's job specification and training might be to undertake all the essential tasks of checking people in and out of the hotel, and to keep a very smart appearance. Added to that, they're told that if customer satisfaction scores exceed 80%, they will receive a 10% bonus. *Inspirational* leaders might do both of those things, but in addition they would help colleagues see *why* a great reception makes such a difference. For example, they would explore with the receptionist the importance of first impressions, and how the reception greeting is at the heart of that. They might discuss how guests arrive tired from a long journey with an important business engagement ahead, or perhaps on a long-awaited break that they have saved up for. Whatever the scenario, every guest has his or her own story, and for each of them the reception experience is pivotal, and the best receptionists look for every way possible to create that superb first impression. Offering a 10% bonus does not offer that insight, and will rarely drive that level of dedication.

At its heart, an inspirational organisation expresses very genuinely what it holds to be important, what it cares about and what its core values are. It then helps colleagues connect with those at a personal level. This whole concept became widespread through the 1990's, with companies such as The Body Shop providing outstanding examples, by setting out not just to provide a great product, but also to convince people at a 'Values' level why theirs was the *right* product. In the case of The Body Shop this was by extolling the virtues of animal rights, and customers and staff alike bought the message, and bought the products. It was in this decade that Steve Jobs rejoined Apple and recommenced his mission to transform the way individuals (as opposed to large corporations) could access and use technology. Few people had Jobs' capability to inspire people with their product; in fact, the *'i'* that precedes all the Apple products refers to the word 'inspire' ... as well as 'individual' and 'internet'. In doing so, Jobs ensured his Apple colleagues knew precisely what the purpose of their endeavours were, and that proved inspirational to colleagues and customers alike.

In terms of leadership thinking, creating a genuine connection between a organisation's values and the values of its employees was a core component of what James McGregor Burns called 'transformational leadership', a style of leadership that truly transforms people and their performance. Burns' model suggested that these leaders do four things more notably than 'transactional leaders':

- **Individual Consideration** – they recognise that people are individuals, take the time and trouble to connect with them personally, become aware of their needs, and focus on their strengths. As a result, they connect closely and rapidly with colleagues.

- **Intellectual Stimulation** – they challenge the *status quo*, and engage others to do the same, recognising that everyone can contribute ideas. It's saying: "There must be a better way, please help us find it."

- **Inspirational Motivation** – they generate enthusiasm by demonstrating that colleagues matter and are an intrinsic part of the organisation's success, and in response achieving the organisation's vision genuinely matters to colleagues too.

- **Idealised Influence** – they are clear about and true to their values, beliefs and convictions, and this authenticity accelerates the process of connecting with and influencing colleagues.

What is so notably different in moving to the *Inspiration* style is that there is no mention of money, or indeed generally of *any* extrinsic motivators. Instead, the emerging transformational leaders were far more interested in the impact of 'intrinsic' motivators i.e. those that lie within you. You are intrinsically motivated when something genuinely matters to you, just like the brilliant hotel receptionist we talked about earlier. If something genuinely matters to a person, it stimulates a different level of performance, which rarely ebbs and flows. Instead, intrinsic motivators are proven to endure far longer than extrinsic motivators, and they have one other spectacular advantage.

Applying extrinsic motivators in a fair and objective way requires you to specify precisely what you want someone to achieve; everyone knows the 'S' of SMART stands for 'specific'. However, you simply cannot fully detail anybody's role, and it is even harder to specify 'quality'. Take our hotel receptionist's role, one that you might think is relatively straightforward to define, but think again. There aren't a 101 activities that will define a brilliant receptionist, nor 1001, nor possibly even 1,000,001. There is an infinite array of scenarios that a receptionist might encounter, and how they gauge the situation, the precise knowledge and skills they call upon to deal with it, and the emotional intelligence and inter-personal skills they bring to the 'how' they deal with the situation all create performance permutations you simply cannot predict or measure on a neat scale. How do you reward the Receptionist who remains alert to guests arriving and takes it upon himself to dash out with an umbrella if it's raining, or who pulls up a weed growing outside the entrance as he arrives for work, or pulls a funny face at a kid who's looking fed up? They are random acts that never make it to a job description, but they have a huge performance impact, and intrinsically motivated employees do it for no other reason than 'it matters'! We'll look further at the impact of connecting Personal and Corporate values in Chapter 3.

🔆 Reflection Point:

Don't get too hung up on fully-SMART objectives. Using a play on the name of popular confectionery brands we suggest goals, instead of always being *SMARTies*, can very often more simply be *M&M's*, the *M's* standing for 'Motivational' and 'Measurable'. In essence, if your colleagues are genuinely motivated to do well in their roles, and you can agree some reasonable metrics to measure performance, then your goal setting is in good shape.

4. Inclusion (aka Co-Creation):

Returning to Aristotle's styles of ruling society, today, more than ever, we see an increased pull towards *democratic* leadership. Indeed, at a national level people lay down their lives for democracy. So it's the dream ticket, the ruling style that all countries around the world are gradually shifting towards, right? Wrong! Establishing a strong democracy is a huge challenge. Indeed, the World Economic Forum reported in Feb 2017 upon Economist Intelligence Unit data regarding democratic factors such as electoral processes, civil liberties and functioning of government, and concluded that: "democracy is in decline", with only 19 countries adjudged to be 'full democracies'. Democracy gives everyone a say, but the trouble is everybody's voice has to be paid attention to, and then massaged into a perfect consensus. That is impossible, because compromise inevitably demands sacrifice, no-one getting precisely what they want. Added to that, public opinion can always be 'moulded' through factors such as logical argument, 'spin', charisma, bribery or even coercion. Whilst democracy may seem like the dream ticket, it has its own flaws like every other system, and it is not difficult to see why the Ancient Greeks themselves were cautious and selective in the application of democracy. Indeed, the first recorded democracy established in Athens around 500BC allowed only about 10-20% of the population to cast their vote.

How does this notion of democracy translate to the workplace? Whilst employment conditions do remain tough for many, the fact is employees today more so than ever have a choice. If necessary, they will vote directly with their feet to exercise that choice, especially those who are most confident and marketable. Thus, to ensure sustainable high performance, the more enlightened organisations recognise the benefits of having everyone fully engaged and contributing all their talents. These are factors that simply cannot be achieved in a domineering environment.

In his 1989 book, *Zapp! The Lightening of Empowerment*, William Byham offered a fable about how empowering people 'zapps' them, whilst not doing so 'saps' them. The book was ahead of its time and became a best-seller, with the story's hero, Joe Mode, recognising that to empower people he had to build others' self-esteem, show empathy, share thoughts and feelings, and strike out and ask others for their help and involvement. This process of 'empowering' people seemed new at the time, but there is still too little evidence of it in workplaces. Leaders take note, more people need to be *zapped*!

Through this empowerment and high levels of inclusion, people have a voice, so are fully involved and able to contribute all their talents, and have a say in what they do and how they do it. You have to know your colleagues and apply good judgement of course, but the end point is, when you trust people, they naturally want to prove you right. So never miss a good opportunity to trust and empower.

"Trusting you was MY choice. Proving me right is YOUR choice."
Anon

Delighted to be Invited

Encouraging this ever-increasing level of *inclusion* has become a hallmark of today's best leaders for numerous reasons:

All aspects of life have become increasingly complex – did you know, for example, that the T&C's of the Apps on an average smartphone contain more words than the Bible's New Testament? No wonder we require the input of so many people with a range of specialist skills for so many of our tasks.

Organisational structures are increasingly matrixed, with people being accountable for contributing to a number of teams. This places further emphasis on people coming together to bring their piece of the jigsaw.

The gradual shift towards remote working, working across sites, and working from home can lead to increased feelings of isolation. Leaders need to counteract this by helping to connect both themselves with their colleagues, and also their colleagues with each other and, in doing so, accept that at times they will be out-of-the-loop.

Generational studies show clearly that the younger generations feel they have something to add and expect to have a voice. Today's pace of change continues to rocket, and as it does the life-expectancy of knowledge continues to plummet. As a result, inexperience is becoming less of a disadvantage, whilst being at the forefront of developments becomes more of an advantage. This 'scissor movement' is good news for the younger generations and good news for all of us, *as long as those around them are wise enough to listen*!

Research invariably shows that 'commitment' levels correlate closely with 'inclusion' levels. It's simple, when we feel we have been consulted we are more likely to be bought-in.

Accountability levels correlate closely with inclusion levels. If it was your idea, even in part, you won't drop the ball.

Thus, inclusive leaders live by the motto: *"None of us is as smart as all of us."* This book will stay true to the principle that the absolute core of leadership is getting the best out of people, which in all but the most short-term or crisis situations will require a spirit of respect, inclusion, appreciation, support, and healthy challenge. In its most practical sense, it involves upping the level of *dialogue* in your organisation, the Greek word combining *dia*: meaning 'through', and *logos*: meaning 'reason', and is therefore the process of sharing thoughts. It is an engaging style of leadership that makes people want to join an organization and turn up enthusiastically every day to give their best, go the extra mile, support the team, develop their talents, and stay long term.

"It doesn't make sense to hire smart people and then tell them what to do. We hired smart people so they could tell us what to do." Steve Jobs

It is right to seek evidence to support the validity of these emerging leadership trends. So much research continues to emerge that both supports highly inclusive leadership and exposes the pitfalls of 'sole leadership'. For example, a 2016 report from Erasmus University Rotterdam, entitled: *We are (all) the Champions*, demonstrates that "status ... has an inverted U-shaped relationship with project quality", meaning that whilst initially the quality of projects rises in line with the status of the person(s) responsible, that correlation eventually peaks, beyond which the correlation flips to 'inverse', in that further increased status leads to a lower quality output. The report cites many reasons for this, including that high-status people are less drawn to seek others' input or approval; they are less likely to be challenged when things are going wrong due to reluctance or admiration; and they have greater authority and influence to secure ongoing project funding and support even in the face of obvious failings. These factors all endorse today's inclusive approach, that encourages leaders to hear others' opinions and to benefit from their open and honest feedback and contribution.

"You talk and talk, until 'the talk' starts." American Indian saying

Far from the domineering 'Push' styles of leadership that result in a culture of compliance, today's inspiring and inclusive leaders focus on 'Pull', which drives commitment levels up. And one thing is for sure; 'commitment beats compliance' every day of the week!

Reflection Point:

The Japanese have a cautionary saying: *Issho ko narite bankotsu karu,* meaning 'A general's success is built on the bones of ten thousand soldiers'. It is a reminder to the upper echelons that they are not the sole reason for their company's success and they should not take all the credit. It takes an entire organisation of dedicated people to deliver success. The best leaders 'get' that, and work hard to create an organisation where everyone has an emotional and financial connection to overall success. It shows in their inclusivity, respect, and approach to distributing rewards. They are the 'co-creators', they have the inside track, and trust me, they *will* win!

Creating a Great Workplace 2

Until its privatisation in 1987, Japan Airlines was government-owned for more than three decades. Despite the privatisation, the airline continued to struggle, eventually entering bankruptcy protection at the start of 2010. In response, the board appointed a new CEO, 77-year-old Kazuo Inamori. Although a hugely successful businessman, having founded the Kyocera corporation 50 years earlier, he had no experience of running an airline business. Undaunted, he says his biggest challenge was to change JAL's *"rigid and bureaucratic"* corporate culture. How did he do it? Inamori explains, *"My simple philosophy is to make all the staff happy. It has been my golden rule since I founded Kyocera. Not to make shareholders happy, but simply to create the company that every employee is proud to work for."* It was a philosophy that had served the former Buddhist monk well throughout his business career.

Amongst his business practices, the quietly spoken CEO had a preferred way of connecting with his people, and learning about the business. *"I brought six cans of beer after sessions or to people who were working late,"* he says. *"After a beer or two, people opened up and told me their honest opinions."* The tactic is known as *nommunication* in Japan, a term that mixes the verb *nomu*, meaning 'to drink', with the word 'communication'. Inamori believes these informal chats provide the most powerful insights a CEO can receive. It seems he is right, Mr Inamori's methods led to JAL's rapid turnaround and relisting on the Tokyo Stock Exchange, his concluding words being: *"It really feels that all of our employees are united now, which is the key to the company's revival."* Mr Inamori has since moved on to the Chairman's role, and when questioned about his choice of successor, Yoshiharu Ueki a pilot of 35-years-experience but little as a business manager, he replied *"I appointed Mr Ueki because of his personality; I think he has a wonderful character. If he ever finds it difficult to decide, I think he will come and talk to me, even when I'm retired."*

Whether you choose to share out the beers like Mr Inamori, or prefer coffee machine chats or a stroll in the park, the 'walk the floor' management technique is about getting amongst colleagues, and chatting informally to them within their workspace. The sense of connectivity that this generates between those at the 'top' of the organization and those at the 'front', will pay untold dividends. It is not the panacea to creating a great workplace, but it is a fabulous start.

The Utopian workplace

The concept of 'utopia' derives from the Greek words 'ou' (not) and 'topos' (place), and was first used by Sir Thomas More in 1516 in his essay of that name, in which he described an imaginary idyllic island called Utopia in the mid-Atlantic, where everybody worked and lived happily alongside each other in perfect social conditions. Just as More's chosen title implied that in reality 'no place' enjoyed such perfect conditions, we too have to accept that that reality extends to our workplaces. Some people, for example, place an emphasis on freedom & flexibility, others on organisation and clarity; some on fairness of pay and team-orientation, others on high rewards for outstanding contributors; some want risk and adventure, others want stability and security etc. Therefore, no one place can possibly be utopia for everyone.

If a 'great workplace' is not, or more to the point *cannot* be *Utopia*, then what can it be? Perhaps the answer lies in the work of 18th Century philosopher Jeremy Bentham who believed 'the greatest happiness of the greatest number is the foundation of morals and legislation'. This almost mathematical assessment led Bentham to propose that actions can be assessed as either good or evil based upon how much pleasure and pain they cause, and to how many people. The logic is compelling, however, can we really accurately measure the opposing impacts of our actions and fairly judge whether the positive outcomes justify the negative? Perhaps more importantly, what about the rights of individuals, those for whom the actions will cause pain? Can we live comfortably imposing huge 'pain' upon a small number in order to grant moderate 'pleasure' for the masses?

That said, we cannot just give up on the idea of a great workplace, with the lame excuse: "You can't please all the people all of the time", because you *can* please most of the people most of the time by creating a friendly and stimulating environment, in other words, a positive workplace. Prof Pierre Casse from Solvay Business School defined leadership by saying: *"Leaders create an environment where people can perform, grow and enjoy."* The three factors he highlights in his definition are powerful criteria for determining whether yours is a great place to work. The consensus from various research initiatives is that leadership within a workplace accounts for 70% of the 'climate', and so all other factors that might influence a climate add up to 30%. By 'climate' they mean *'how it feels to work here'*, and Casse's definition helps committed leaders focus their attention on the three following critical components of their working environment. Does your workplace:

• Enable colleagues to apply all their talents and energies to best effect. (Perform)

• Offer development opportunities that encourage them to improve. (Grow)

• Ensure people feel positive about the day-to-day interactions. (Enjoy)

If your team would rate each of these criteria as 'high', then congratulations, you have created a great place to work. And the predictable result is your fully-utilised, ever-improving and happy colleagues will show more commitment than the rest, which will consistently feed to the bottom line. A joint study in 2014 between Wharton (US) and Warwick (UK) Business Schools concluded, "employee satisfaction is associated with positive abnormal [stock] returns" and similarly, when reviewing the financial performance of companies that feature within 'Best Companies To Work For" lists, the evaluations routinely point to top-tier stock returns. It is hardly a surprise that positive people generate great results, but it is well worth banging on about.

Casse's three environmental components go some way to helping understand an organisation's 'culture', in other words *'how things get done around here'*. Yet, whilst we talk most commonly about 'organisational culture', we ignore the fact that cultures exist most tangibly within individual teams and departments. There may be a few organisational characteristics that apply commonly, and influence the wider culture, but they are usually over-shadowed in terms of 'how the workplace feels' for each individual by 'local' cultural influences. There is no single way of life, no uniform culture, that permeates an entire organisation. Instead, corporate cultures operate on a far more local level, with individual team leaders driving their own cultural agendas. It is those leaders who most significantly influence people's immediate surroundings and therefore their experience of the workplace.

Let's look at ways in which leaders can create a 'great' workplace.

Create 'meaning' in roles

In the previous chapter we talked about *Inspirational* leadership, and the importance of connecting with people's personal values i.e. what's important to them, and the benefits of using that knowledge to ensure their job contributes to satisfying those. Doing this creates a clearer sense of meaning to people's roles. It may seem an obvious point, but sadly all the evidence points to too few employees having much sense of their role being meaningful. A Harvard Business Review survey in 2013 revealed that half the respondents felt their job had no 'meaning and significance', and numerous other surveys which similarly reveal depressingly small percentages of people who actually 'like their job'.

But there is hope for those leaders who don't accept such statistics are inevitable, because at the other end of the scale those same surveys continually show that around 20% of people are 'very fulfilled' in their jobs. And those fortunate people span a wide-variety of jobs and organisational levels, so the difference

29

in satisfaction levels cannot be attributed to the nature of the job or its seniority. Rather, it's each individual's personal sense of connection and meaning that determines how satisfied they are with their job.

Everyone in a business is a cog in the machine; every cog plays its part, and if one fails, the whole machine fails. So, ensure *all* team members fully understand why their individual contribution is so critical to their team and the business.

Good people create good workplaces

"Let no one ever come to you without leaving better and happier." Mother Teresa

Leadership guru Warren Bennis once quipped *"...leadership is like beauty, hard to define but you know it when you see it,"* and that is largely true. The same concept applies to the notion of a 'good person'. We will look at many aspects of being a 'good person' throughout this book, all of which come together to determine 'what it is like working for you'. For example, would colleagues say that you are consistent and authentic, that you communicate clearly what you stand for and what's expected? Are you fair and considerate, taking time to get to know colleagues and show your appreciation of people's efforts? Do you act with kindness whenever appropriate? Do you set high standards and positively encourage people to reach them, whilst tackling under-performance in an honest and constructive way? And, do you 'walk-the-walk', by role modelling your own standards?

If you display those qualities, the impact on workplace satisfaction and retention is profound. A mantra within HR circles goes: "People join a company, but leave a boss." Accordingly, dissatisfaction with a line manager is a consistent theme in 'exit interviews', and that is a shame for all concerned. We need to pay far more attention to recruiting and developing leaders who are 'good people'.

Look after your team

Businesses in the 80's and 90's obsessed about *Shareholders* almost to the point that they seemed the only stakeholders who mattered. Then in the 00's, businesses became notably more focused upon *Customers*, the stakeholders who actually pay the bills and allow businesses to keep their shareholders happy. Yet, throughout these decades you would often see companies declaring 'people are our most important asset', although in reality there was scant evidence that this was true. Today however, more companies finally are shifting to recognise *Staff* as critical stakeholders. They are the ones who keep the customers happy, the balance sheet healthy, and therefore the shareholders happy!

Look at the myriad of entrepreneurial businesses springing up around the globe, and note how the common thread that joins so many of them is their massive focus on creating a great workplace experience by genuinely putting their people at the heart of the business. Social media entrepreneur Jamie Bolding claims that a common mistake of businesses is to spend more money, time and attention on their clients than on their employees. Instead, Bolding reckons: "the actual money that's spent on employees should surpass the money spent on your clients. Ultimately the most important people in your business are the people that work in the company."

Looking out for people, so that they look out for you, is entirely rational human behaviour, social psychologists calling it 'The Law of Reciprocity', which asserts that when someone does something positive for you, you have an innate and often subconscious instinct to repay that kindness; put simply, 'you reap what you sow'. Think about someone who surprises you with an unexpected birthday gift; I bet you will be drawn to reciprocate the gift-buying when it is their birthday. The concept is used extensively in the field of Sales, whether it's a gift, a cup of coffee, or a salesperson who puts herself out for you in some way. Whatever it is, an inner-voice will be telling you to return the favour! So, look after your staff, and they'll look after you.

Reciprocity is far from a new concept. For example, I've spent much of my business life staying in hotels, and I can't help but compare experiences. Over many years in the 1990's I noticed how the staff at Marriott hotels always seemed to be empathetic. Trainers like me, who arrive late at night after a long journey and are concerned to ensure the facilities for the following day's event are all in hand, really appreciate a little bit of empathy at check-in, whether that's to allow you a quick glimpse into the conference room you'll be using, or to let you know who will be available to help you in the morning, and what time they arrive etc. The Marriott staff always seemed to 'get' that. In the bedrooms at many of the Marriott venues was a copy of *Marriott's Way*, a book by J.W. Marriott Jr, telling how the family hotel business had grown from one outlet to the global organisation it now is. It was an interesting read, but the bit that stood out for me was the founder's philosophy that had underpinned the business from day one: *"If we look after our people, they'll look after our customers."* Simple, yet supremely effective!

And Marriott are far from alone in this approach. It turns out that the well-worn cliché: *"It's nice to be important, but it's more important to be nice"* is absolutely true. Canadian hotelier, Isadore "Issy" Sharp founded Four Seasons Hotels back in 1960, and remains close to the day-to-day running of the $4bn p.a. chain. Whilst many factors contribute to that sort of success, Issy has always been clear that the #1 success factor has been offering the best possible service, and that, he believes, is only possible when staff are happy. He comments: *"It comes down to one principle that transcends time and geography, religion and culture. It's the golden rule – do unto others as you would want done to you. It is the simple idea that if you treat people well ... they will do the same."* Four Seasons is renowned for both its exceptional service levels and its low staff turnover rates, and has featured every year since inception in Fortune magazine's '100 Best Companies to Work For'. Let's raise a glass to Issy and to 'being nice'!

Step Up or Step Out

The best leaders are fully aware of how even a small contingent can disrupt the positive atmosphere, so never compromise on high behavioural standards. In James Kerr's book *Legacy*, about the leadership lessons from New Zealand's world-beating All Blacks rugby team, he shares the team's rather unsubtle mantra, "No D*ckheads". If you've ever managed a team with even just one 'rotten apple' you know the impact that person can have. In line with the recruitment maxim: "Recruit in haste, repent at leisure", the All Blacks are the epitome of a 'high performing team' and they understand how quickly team cohesion can be undermined if even one player fails to live up to their code of behaviour. For example, the entire squad believe in 'sweeping the sheds', which means looking after yourself and even the most menial tasks, and not expecting others to do it for you. Former player Andrew Mehrtens explains it: *"Because no one looks after the All Blacks, the All Blacks look after themselves"*, and the longest-serving captain Sean Fitzpatrick summarises it less-delicately: *"Front up, or f**k off."* There's no space for passengers or prima donnas in the All Black set-up, and their no-nonsense philosophy is what secures their exceptional culture.

It's good to talk

A story emerged a number of years ago, supposedly from the New York Times, about a guy named George Turklebaum. George was a proof-reader at a New York firm, and reportedly was found dead at his office desk one Saturday morning when a cleaner tried to ask him why he was working at the weekend. What was most shocking about the story was that a post mortem revealed he had died of a heart attack about 5 days beforehand. Despite working in an open plan office with 23 other workers, simply no-one noticed George was dead, for an entire week. His boss, Elliot Wachiaski, was reported as saying: 'George was always the first guy in each morning and the last to leave at night, so no-one found it unusual that he was in the same position all that time and didn't say anything. He was always absorbed in his work and kept much to himself.'

You may well have heard the story too, and hopefully you also now know it was a somewhat curious hoax, emanating from the internet not from the New York Times. It took a long time to be cleared up, but in the meantime it sparked a whole heap of debate about just how little attention some workers get. Indeed, one police officer who was questioned about the story's validity commented that whilst he could not confirm it, he knew of other such cases including one where a worker had died in the workplace 18 days before being found. I don't know whether that story is true or hoax either, but let's accept the intended message that we should take the time and trouble to stay well-connected with our people.

The debate that followed was, I suppose, what the hoaxer had hoped to generate, as it got people talking about whether our workplaces are inclusive and friendly, or whether they are cold and detached. As we will discuss in Chapter 7, under the subject of *Strokes*, 'being recognised' is what psychologists consider the most basic human need. We are instantly buoyed by a nod or a "Hi" or a hug, just as we are offended or hurt by being ignored. In some African cultures they have a greeting that goes *"I am here to be seen"*, and the person you are meeting replies: *"I see you"*; it's consistent in every culture that we all want to be visible and be recognised.

In the main, we recognise people by showing our appreciation of them. "It's good to see you"; "Thanks for supporting the project yesterday"; "I appreciate your feedback on the report"; "Thanks for those customer service suggestions"; "I like your new haircut" etc. It's not shallow: it's essential. It feeds our relationships, it creates a positive spirit, and it frees people to be natural and to work in their 'flow'.

"I have yet to find the man, however exalted his station, who did not do better work and put forth greater effort under a spirit of approval than under a spirit of criticism." Charles M. Schwab

Happiness is not enough

Data from research such as Gallup's April 2017 workplace culture survey continues to highlight the business benefits of getting culture right, such as reduced absenteeism, lower staff turnover, improved customer satisfaction, increased sales, and increased profitability. However, a cautionary note is needed here, because such surveys also warn us not to focus exclusively on 'employee happiness'. There are plenty of happy people who are also unproductive!

What workplace surveys also show is that creating really high performance cultures depends upon employee requirements much more expansive than solely 'happiness' being met, such as those suggested below by Gallup:

- Do employees feel they have a stake in the organisation's future?
- Are work expectations clearly and fairly established?
- Do employees have sufficient resources to do their work?
- Do employees receive sufficient training and development?
- Are efforts made to ensure good relationships amongst co-workers?
- All that said, you have to start somewhere, and 'happiness' isn't a bad start!

Vary your Leadership

In the 1960's Paul Hersey and Ken Blanchard produced the well-known *Situational Leadership* framework which helped leaders consider different styles of leadership, each being appropriate in different circumstances depending upon the 'development stage' of the people being led. In other words, the 'best way' to lead depended primarily upon the given situation. Drilling deeper, the model should be applied not just to each individual, but also to differing aspects of an individual's work. There may be aspects within people's roles where they are the industry expert and thus a 'hands off' style of leadership might well be most appropriate, yet other aspects where they are inexperienced, and so a more 'hands on' style of leadership is likely to be more effective. Earlier models, such as Robert Blake & Jane Mouton's *Managerial Grid* similarly proposed that leaders vary their styles, in this case depending upon their degree of concern for 'people' versus their concern for 'production'.

The consistent message though is simple; leaders have to vary their style to fit the situation. The 'situational' model 'FAB', standing for Front, Alongside, and Behind, is extremely helpful in our discussions with aspiring leaders to identify what their preferred style is, and whether they lean too heavily on this 'default' style. Regardless, we review each of the styles and the benefits each offers, and in doing so encourage greater flexibility.

In essence, **Front** leaders are inclined to set direction and pace, often adopting an authoritative and assertive approach. They motivate others through their overt energy and role modelling, 'beating the drum' to encourage others along. It can be powerful and inspiring, and both history and corporate life are littered with remarkable acts of leading from the front, when a leader steps up and demonstrates a personal commitment and belief in the way forward. It can be especially effective in a crisis, or when colleagues need that clear steer. Indeed, it's hard to imagine an effective leader who was unable to lead, at times, from the Front.

However, be careful if Front is your *only* style of leading, because it eventually leaves others feeling drained and demotivated, and your confident and authoritative style tips over the edge, becoming dictatorial and oppressive. Performance sinks as a result.

The **Alongside** leaders are far more adept at rolling their sleeves up and helping their colleagues, paying minimal attention to hierarchy, and instead just 'being a colleague'. As a result, they become closely connected and alert to the support each needs at any point, including taking account of personal issues. There is a leadership saying: *"Before you can lead someone you have to get alongside them"*, and this was epitomised by Lawrence of Arabia who led the Arab Bedouin tribes during WW1, gaining heroic status amongst his men not least because he learned their language, lived cheek-by-cheek with them in accordance with their traditions, and always demanded more of himself than he expected from his men. He was famously described by one of the Arab sheikh leaders: *"Of all the men I have met, Al Aurans (the Arabs' name for Lawrence) was the greatest prince"*. Few things endear leaders to their teams more than the willingness to put their status aside and just 'muck in'. The Chinese proverb: *"A thousand candles can be lit from a single candle, and the life of the candle will not be shortened. Happiness never decreases by being shared"* reflects well the incredible impact an 'alongside' leader can have. It's a style that builds trust and respect, and sets the leader up to be an effective coach. Leaders who lack the ability to 'get alongside' their colleagues never build the inter-personal bonds and trust that underpin effective team working, and that lack of engagement costs them dearly.

However, if it is your *only* style of leading, the team may eventually become suspicious that you lack the vision and passion of a Front leader, or that you only stay closely involved in everything the team does because you don't trust their capability or commitment to perform without you being present. Ultimately, the team may even question more fundamentally *why* you are the leader.

Leading from **Behind** is a powerful style when leading a highly experienced, skilled and motivated team. Usually, high performing teams like that will tell you the best thing you can do as a leader is 'get the heck out of the way'! In the 2017 Russian F1 Grand Prix, leading and with eight laps to go, Mercedes driver Valtteri Bottas coolly said over the team radio *"I want less talking"*. The team director understood, and with less information distracting him Bottas held on to claim his maiden F1 victory. Paradoxically, it takes high self-confidence for a leader to take a step back because, at least in that instance, it's an acknowledgement that the leader has no role, or worse, he's not even wanted. Indeed, his people on many occasions are able to perform better without his interference. Far from revealing a leadership failing, it's a reflection of great recruitment, development and empowerment; don't fear it, enjoy it!

The classic leadership style that encapsulates this approach is Coaching, where the leader questions and listens, but avoids giving answers or advice. It represents a huge demonstration of respect and trust from the leader, is closely aligned to the concept of empowerment, and research points to this approach being hugely successful when used appropriately. The saying, *"Leaders become their most powerful when they give their power away"*, summarises the positive effect of getting the Behind style right. Leaders who lack the trust or good sense to lead from Behind when appropriate, deprive their colleagues of some of the best learning opportunities and the satisfaction of having been empowered, and deprive themselves of welcome headspace. Instead, they are busy trying to preserve and promote their leadership position, which is a drag on everyone else.

However, if Behind is your *only* style of leading, the team may eventually become suspicious about the motivation level of their distant and detached leader, wondering whether you even care about the team. Eventually the team learn to by-pass their leader and operate independently, or even seek the guidance of other leaders in adjacent or relevant roles. It's OK to be 'hands off', but it's not OK to be 'written off'!

The table overleaf sets out the key traits and skills exhibited by each type of leader, and the behaviours & phrases that they might more commonly use:

Front

Traits & Skills:	Behaviours & *Phrases*:
Setting Direction	Standing up to make presentations
Presenting a compelling Vision	Offering personal reassurances
Setting an example	Displaying confidence and assertiveness
Courage of convictions	Rallying the troops
Personal accountability	*"Follow me ... get on the bus"*
Encourage/enforce compliance	*"We can do it"*
'Walking the Walk'	*"This will happen"*

Alongside

Traits & Skills:	Behaviours & *Phrases*:
Relationship building	All hands on deck
Coaching (*from the 'side line'*)	Building on ideas
Personal Support	Together we can do it
Concern for individuals	If one fails, we all fail
Friendliness	*"What does everyone think?"* ... *"Can anyone help here?"* ... *"How can I help?"*
Openness and vulnerability	*"Who has experience of this?"*

Behind

Traits & Skills:	Behaviours & *Phrases*:
Delegating (not abdicating!)	I need you to take this on ... I know you can rise to the challenge.
Coaching (*from the 'stands'*)	*"You make the decisions, but I'm here for you if needed"*
Empowering	
Challenging	The only way to make someone trustworthy, is to trust them!
Supporting	Operates 'behind the scenes'

Action Point:

The FAB model gives leaders the insights and framework needed to avoid being a leadership 'one trick pony'. After all, if the only tool you have is a hammer, then you will treat everything like a nail. The tongue-in-cheek leadership advice below highlights the pitfalls of choosing the wrong the style:

Do not walk behind me, for I may not lead. Do not walk ahead of me, for I may not follow. Do not walk beside me, for the path is narrow. In fact, just sod off and leave me alone! Anon

Instead, the most successful people in life have the most choice of approach, and know when to use them. So, make sure you adapt your FAB style appropriately, and there is rarely a better way to do that than to ask your team how they view your style, and whether they would appreciate any modifications. Ultimately, the choice is yours, but considering their views at least means your choice is informed, and is in itself a demonstration of inclusive leadership.

Imagine the power of an organisation that has truly created a great place to work, in which 100% of the employees were 'very fulfilled' and 'fully engaged'. Create that vibe amongst your tribe and watch results soar!

"Those are my principles,
and if you don't like them.
well, I have others."

Groucho's quote is a sharp elbow in the ribs to those who profess to holding something as important, but then do a U-turn the minute it is advantageous to do so. Knowing what's truly important to you, and standing by those values is a mark of a consistent and authentic leader.

We don't all have to have identical values of course, but knowing what our leaders stand for and knowing that they stay true to that is something we all admire. Building upon that, leaders who take an interest in other people's values, and respect and support them in satisfying their values, are elevated to the top tier of those in the leadership field.

True Sportsmanship

Eugenio Monti is one of the most celebrated bobsleigh athletes of all time. Having won two silver medals at his first Olympics in 1956 in his home country of Italy, unfortunately, the 1960 Winter Olympics did not host a bobsleigh event. So Monti had to continue training and waiting for eight years, until the 1964 Innsbruck Olympics, to attempt his dream of achieving Gold.

Joint favourites going into the 1964 Innsbruck Games were the local Austrians and Monti's Italians. After the first heat however, the Canada 1 crew took the lead having broken the Olympic record, but in doing so had also broken their axle. Unless they could repair the damaged parts in time, Canada 1 faced disqualification. It was a moment that would define Monti's career and reputation. Unwilling to benefit from what he saw as an 'unfair' advantage, Monti and his mechanics set about repairing the Canadian's seized axle. With Monti's help, Canada 1 continued through the competition, and won the coveted Gold, with Eugenio Monti and his team achieving Bronze.

Undeterred, Monti set about achieving his dream of Gold in the two-man Bobsled event, but the same dilemma was about to strike. The British team, having recorded the fastest time for the first run, had sheared a bolt attaching the runners to the sled. Eugenio once again did not hesitate to do what he considered to be the 'right thing', removing the necessary bolt from his sled and sending it immediately to the British team. With the help of Monti's bolt, the British pair of Tony Nash and Robin Dixon won Gold, whilst Monti and his two-man partner again took the Bronze, and later were awarded the "Pierre de Coubertin" award for fair play. Quizzed by Italian journalists about his actions, Monti simply explained: "Nash didn't win because I gave him the bolt, he won because he had the fastest run."

Monti's achievements did not stop there. At 40-years-old Monti entered his final Olympics, the 1968 Grenoble games. In what were surely the two most loudly-applauded medal ceremonies, Monti and his Italian team mates won Gold in both the two-man and four-man events. His Olympic dream had finally been achieved, and to top it all he was awarded Italy's highest civilian honour, the Commendatore of the Italian Republic. "Salute, Eugenio!"

Personal Values

The story of Eugenio Monti gives us a great insight into the impact of personal values, and how core they are to our behaviours i.e. those daily actions we take that define *who we are*. There will be some who would take the view that Eugenio was in a competitive sport, and part of that was about preparation of your equipment for all eventualities; and so why should those who failed to have a contingency plan in place benefit from a competitor who had? It's a perfectly reasonable view, but it wasn't Eugenio's.

Psychologists broadly agree that our values and beliefs i.e. what is important to us and what is right and wrong, are shaped by around the age of seven. The finer details of course won't be formed until later in life, but the fundamental building blocks will be. This view accords with the Jesuit maxim: *"Give me the boy til he's seven, and I'll show you the man."* These early-forming values develop and deepen as we enter adulthood, and shape the way we choose to live our lives. Whether, for example, you have an outlook of 'you only have one life, so live it', or an outlook of 'life is a long-haul, so you must plan for a secure future' will clearly shape the person that you are, either towards someone who is drawn to 'enjoying the moment' or to 'building for the future'.

The role of a leader is not to judge others' personal values. After all, the clue is in the word, they're 'personal'! That said, a well-intended discussion around 'does that work for you?' and 'might you consider re-assessing that value?' very often is a helpful leadership intervention. But what is useful is to help people consider whether what they are doing i.e. how they live their life, is supporting them achieving their personal values. A colleague of mine came up with a great insight, saying: "If you want to know what's important to someone, you only need to look at two books; their diary and their cheque book. Whatever else they may say, how they spend their time and their money reveals what is most important to them." So, the person who insists 'Family is #1 to me', yet is self-oriented, regularly socialises after work and at home is glued to the TV, PC and Smartphone, is kidding both you and himself. Now you may be thinking that you have no right to interfere with another's values, however a courageous and well-intended leader might well disagree. You see, because values form early and are so deeply embedded we often lose sight of them. The person who loves her parents dearly and places a high value on being a caring daughter, can nonetheless get caught up in the 'busy-ness' of life, and before she knows it the opportunity to show her love and gratitude disappears. Or the person who has always wanted to apply their creative side, but has just never explored how that could be accommodated in their life. As a result, we 'lose our way', and fail to use our time effectively to satisfy those values. Having a conversation with colleagues about what they value, and how you can support them retaining or regaining their focus, is high-impact leadership.

"The mind can be convinced, but the heart must be won." Simon Sinek

💡 Action Point:

Take the time to write down your own values. I did, 15 years ago, and they're shown below to give you an idea:

External/Others:	Personal:
Help Family to flourish	Open to Experience
Be Positive	Keep Fit & Healthy
Show Integrity	Make time for Myself
Be Reliable	Self-Esteem is OK
Be a 'Giver'	Enjoy Today!!

They've shifted a little over time but I'm glad I made the list, and it did keep them in focus and help me towards achieving them. My advice is to share them with colleagues - I've found that helpful over the years, and have gained also from insights into others' values. For example, I have a colleague whose values include 'never gossip' and 'be a friend', both of which he adheres to admirably and that inspires me too.

Leading through Values

"Every man should view himself as equally balanced: half good and half evil. Likewise, he should see the entire world as half good and half evil...With a single good deed he will tip the scales for himself, and for the entire world, to the side of good." Rabbi Maimonides, 12th Century Philosopher

In Chapter 1, we mentioned the importance of leaders being clear about and true to their values, beliefs and convictions. James McGregor Burns' model of 'transformational leadership' described this aspect of leadership as *Idealised Influence*, and leaders who demonstrated this clarity and consistency were seen as authentic and having integrity, and that enhanced their ability to connect with and influence colleagues.

However, the best leaders go beyond being clear about their own values, by taking a genuine interest in what's important to those they lead, and actively helping their colleagues to satisfy those values. Doing so has a massive impact upon any relationship, whether at work or in our personal lives, and *values-based leaders* know this. In our leadership consultancy, we facilitate the process of achieving this in three stages, generally finding it best to do so in an informal team setting to encourage openness and trust.

1. The first step is to identify what everyone's values are, and we use a range of exercises, from 'quick & fun' to 'thorough & considered', that prompt people to identify their values, and to rank how important each is to them. Whilst you might imagine that everyone is fully-aware of their own values, because they

tend to be held deep within us, actually most people cannot instantly 'access' them. So, the exercises are worthwhile from a self-awareness perspective alone. We then ask people to describe what they mean by that value; *economic security* to some people means to be able to put food on the table, whilst to others it means to build a very comfortable pension alongside a well-funded investment portfolio. To some, *enjoyment* means to have a job that they are contented with, to others it's to be part of a fun team that socialise a lot, whilst earning sufficient to pay for several ski trips a year.

2. The second step is to ask people to assess to what extent their values are being satisfied in the context of their working life, using either a 1-10 score or a Red-Amber-Green ranking. I suggest limiting this to say their 'top three' values, to keep the conversation focused. Again, the output of this stimulates great conversation as people explain their ratings and the team have the opportunity to enquire and contribute their thoughts about what might improve the satisfaction ratings. As an example, I had a colleague who expressed *uniqueness* and *creativity* as two of his top values; first, I would never have known that without the exercise, but secondly, I was then able to find opportunities for him to express himself more and have greater involvement in the creative stages of our team's projects. The outcome was really positive for both him and the team.

3. The third step moves beyond the team session, and involves the leader and each colleague in a 1:1 setting. The first message is 'thank you for sharing what's important to you', because that alone leaves both parties feeling much better connected. And the objective then becomes to explore, 'how can I help you satisfy those values?' In our experience there are always steps you can take to tailor every role so that it enhances the satisfaction of personal values. If you do this, and are genuine in your efforts, you are guaranteed fabulous relationships with fully committed colleagues.

Moral Compass

Consider this dilemma. You are stood by the points of a railway track, holding the lever that controls whether trains fork either left or right at the junction ahead. News has reached you that there is a runaway train approaching at speed, it's brakes have broken, and there is no way to stop it. The points are set to send the train its normal route to the left, where ahead there is a steep decline which will cause the train's speed to increase to the point that it will derail, with a high probably of many passenger fatalities. Alternatively, if you pull the lever so that the train forks to the right, the track eventually reaches an incline that will stop the train, but not before reaching a large group of railway workers working on this section of track. They have no way of anticipating the train, and most probably a high proportion will be killed. What would you do?

It is a classic moral dilemma, with no right or wrong answer. Assuming there is no clever or creative 'third option' available to rescue everyone at danger, it is a straight choice between two awful outcomes. So, what would you do? Whilst *what* you decide is interesting, the fascinating part is *how* you decided; on what *basis* did you make your decision? Was it your best-guess of how many people might be on the train versus how many workers might be on the track? Was it the likelihood of passengers surviving a derailment versus workers being able to leap from the track? Or a personal judgement about the likely age and gender profile of the train passengers compared to the rail workers? Maybe, more fundamentally, you decided you have no right to 'play God' by interfering with the points lever at all, and instead must let fate take its course; philosophers referring to this as the choice between 'acts' and 'omissions'. For example, is it any worse to kill someone than to deliberately fail to save their life? Is it any worse to tell a lie, than to stay silent when you could tell the truth? For some there is a difference, yet for other's such as theologian Blaise Pascale, who declared: *"Silence is the greatest persecution"*, there is not.

These are extreme examples admittedly, but then navigating through our complex lives is never straightforward, and moral dilemmas at some level or other arise all the time. Do you, for example, make a group of colleagues redundant with all the ramifications of that, or do you risk the future of the business and everyone else's jobs by carrying unsustainable costs? Do you promote one colleague over other team members because you see their potential and commitment, even though the other team members are equally high performing at this point? Or switch from a loyal supplier, to one who is prepared to undercut the price to win our business? These dilemmas confront us frequently and, make no mistake, it is our values that form our 'moral compass', and play a bigger part than logic ever does in informing our major decisions. Values-based leaders know what they stand for, and because of that they are consistent and authentic. You may not agree with their values, and you may not agree with their every decision, but you will at least understand them.

The sport of cross country running rarely hits the headlines. However, events at a top international race in Navarre, Spain in December 2012 attracted huge media attention. Kenyan athlete Abel Mutai was approaching the finish line with an unassailable lead over top Spanish runner Ivan Fernandez Anaya, when he mistakenly thought he had crossed the line, so stopped with his hands raised in celebration. He was in fact standing 10 metres short of the line, but was unable to understand the Spanish crowd who sportingly were urging him to carry on. Anaya was now approaching rapidly, but had clearly understood what was happening, and without hesitation placed his hands on Mutai, pushing him over the line to victory. Interviewed afterwards, Anaya took little credit for his actions, explaining: "I didn't deserve to win. I did what I had to do. He was the rightful winner. He created a gap that I couldn't have closed. As soon as I saw he was stopping, I knew I wasn't going to pass him."

The Final Word: The theologian Benjamin Jowett said, *"The real measure of our wealth is how much we'd be worth if we lost all our money"*, and for sure the Monti's and the Anaya's of this world would be worth a lot. Get familiar with your values and stay true to them; they'll serve you well, and make you a better leader.

Section 2:
The Leader's Outlook

Chapters:

4. Embracing Change

5. Taking Risks

6. Positive Attitude

7. Continual Improvement

Embracing Change

Whilst taking a ferry to Norway many years ago, I saw a laid-back looking guy wearing a T-shirt with that slogan on the front, and it made me smile.

My grandfather used to talk endlessly about the 'good old days', yet lived through two World Wars, never owned a house or a car, and worked long hours on a lathe his entire life. As was quite common in those days, he had all his teeth extracted as a young man and never wore dentures, so lived on soft foods! I loved him dearly, but I always mused over his glowing assessment of the past, and how rooted he was to a world that no longer existed.

History is littered with examples of those who resisted change. The Luddites were an affiliated group of English textile workers in the 19th-century who destroyed industrial machinery as a form of protest. They considered the use of such machinery to be "fraudulent and deceitful", aimed at damaging workers' rights. Fearing the skills of their trade would become redundant, the movement grew in scale and expanded nationwide. It was only military force and the tragic shooting of protestors by factory owners that brought the Luddite movement to an end. Around that time, in similar vein, the French verb 'saboter' emerged, deriving from the French word 'sobot', meaning 'clogs', and referring to the French workers' tactic of throwing wooden clogs into machines to damage or destroy them. It is clear that many people are highly resistant to change and invest huge personal time, energy and risk in that resistance. But you can't stand still in today's world, and it is no place for Luddites and saboteurs.

There are few people remaining in any business who would dispute the notion that 'change is a constant' and that it is accelerating exponentially. Yet the human psyche so often rejects or at least resists the need to keep on changing, preferring like my grandfather, to reminisce about the good old days. Why then is change such an ordeal?

William Bridges' must-read book *Managing Transitions: Making the Most of Change* coined the phrase: "It isn't the changes that do you in, it's the transitions", by which he meant the practicalities of the change are one thing, but the real challenges lie in the psychological process that people must go through as they make sense of what the changes mean for them, and how they can best deal with them. The process involves three stages. The first stage centres on our need to *'Let Go'* of whatever we are moving away from; whether that's a physical location, a role, a working relationship or, in an extreme case, the loss of a loved one.

Whilst the scale of those challenges varies hugely, the process is identical; we can only deal with change when we have come to terms with letting go. Once we do that, we enter a phase when we have accepted the need to move on but are not yet 100%

clear about to where and how that will be; Bridges calls it the *'Neutral Zone'*. Depending upon the issue, our feelings in this zone can range from 'excited anticipation' – such as the surprise holiday scenario where you arrive at the airport unsure until check-in where you are going, to 'fear and despair' – such as a scenario where you have accepted you are losing your job but cannot imagine how you will find another, or how you will pay the bills in the meantime. We have to get through this stage psychologically before we can embrace, or at least face, what Bridges calls the *'New Beginning'*. Reaching that point is marked by your ability to focus all your energies on ensuring the change has the best, or the least bad, impact upon you. If our approach to life was entirely logical we would all move instantly to this point, because it is where we can take whatever level of control is possible to influence the outcome. However, having zero emotional connection would make us robotic, and that's neither realistic nor desirable. Nonetheless, reaching the New Beginning point *is* where we start to take some personal control over the change, so we must not let our emotions prevent us from getting to that point and, as leaders, we must encourage others similarly.

Embracing our Uncertain World

The role of a change leader begins at a deep and personal level to discourage a mindset of resistance and negativity, and to encourage one of exploration and open-mindedness. Not all change will be good news for everyone, but routinely resisting change is a waste of time and energy because that change is going to happen anyway, however hard you dig your heels in.

Spencer Johnson's best-seller, *Who Moved My Cheese?*, struck a chord with everyone who experiences change and those who are tasked with leading it, notably, that the things that are most important to us are the most difficult to change – which would include our jobs, as the Luddites demonstrated - and it is often fear that prevents us from change. Yet, as the mice in Johnson's fable found out, trying new directions keeps our options open and presents new opportunities, and therefore is less risky than standing still. Additionally, if we regularly adopt small changes - even if that simply is, for example, walking a different way to work - it makes us more adaptable when bigger changes arise. So, the lesson is, learn to live with change, and enjoy the ride!

It is worth stating that being open to change is far more about a willingness to embrace uncertainty than it is about being able to predict the future. Indeed, it's about accepting that, to a large extent, we can't. Winston Churchill commented: *"The future isn't what it used to be"*, and of course behind the humour there's a serious point; none of us know with certainty what the future will bring. People who offer their support for change on the proviso that you both explain it in detail and reassure them that it will happen precisely as you set out are both unrealistic and unreasonable, the only feasible response being a John McEnroe-style *"You cannot be serious!"* Even the most gifted visionaries have to adjust their forecasts to reflect emerging realities. A CEO of a major organisation I worked with explained how he was always cautious about plans projecting further ahead than 6 months because, beyond that, he believed it's pretty much guess-work.

The reality, or perhaps I should say 'virtual reality', is that our world is entering another period of transformation, a 'Fourth Industrial Revolution'. The World Economic Forum explained this in Jan 2016: "The First Industrial Revolution used water and steam power to mechanise production. The Second used electric power to create mass production. The Third used electronics and information technology to automate production. Now a Fourth Industrial Revolution ... is characterized by a fusion of technologies that is blurring the lines between the physical, digital, and biological spheres." Aside from the changes themselves, the report goes on to assert: "The speed of current breakthroughs has no historical precedent. When compared with previous industrial revolutions, the Fourth is evolving at an exponential rather than a linear pace. Moreover, it is disrupting almost every industry in every country, and the breadth and depth of these changes herald the transformation of entire systems of production, management and governance." Just think of the medical advancements that emerge almost daily, the exciting applications of new 'wonder' materials such as graphene, and the role of 3-D printing, or the impact of driverless cars, not just on our journeys but their wider social impact. For example, who would want to buy, maintain, insure and wash their own car, when a driverless car can be ordered by voice-activated app and arrive at your house within five minutes! Even our diets are set to change, potentially quite radically, for example as we look for more sustainable sources of nutrition; with dung beetles offering twice the protein of beef, and just four crickets offering the same calcium as a glass of milk, we'd better get used to insects in our lunchbox! These are all predictions of course, and who knows precisely how these emerging innovations will impact us, but make no mistake, 'the pace of change is accelerating, exponentially'.

Two commonly-held theories support this ever-present change and uncertainty. First, there's the *Chaos Theory*, which emerged from the field of mathematics and extended way beyond. The fundamental premise is that even tiny changes to conditions within a system can lead to massive variances to outcomes. The notion of the 'butterfly concept' infers that the beat of a butterfly's fragile wings in one part of the world can set off a chain reaction that results in a tornado on the other side of the globe. That example is impossible to prove, but the mathematical evidence for chaos theory is unquestioned. Practical examples include the unpredictable path of a cluster of snooker balls when hit with force. The precise positioning of the balls in relation to each other ball, the subsequent unpredictable colliding of all those snooker balls, and the imperfect surface of the table all make the final outcome impossible to predict.

The second theory is sometimes referred to as *The Black Swan*, from Nassim Nicholas Taleb's book of the same name. Taleb's book shares insights into how rarely we are able to predict future events, because totally unexpected things happen. The concept of the *Black Swan* refers to the discovery of such birds in Australia and the fact that until that moment everyone assumed swans must be white. Why would we have believed any differently when every shred of evidence that existed confirmed that all swans were white? The same premise exists in the investment world, where Taleb presents a convincing case for us being somewhat less-assured about the financial gurus who manage our investments; they too are constantly blindsided by 'black swans', events that no-one could have predicted, which totally scupper their highly-skilled predictions.

All this uncertainty though, does present a fantastic opportunity for leaders. Once you recognise that much of the change we all encounter is unpredictable, you have an enormous advantage. Acknowledging that we simply cannot predict or control most elements of change means we can embrace the chaotic but exciting world we inhabit. The American Psychological Society's advice for dealing with change includes 'keeping things in perspective'; 'nurturing a positive self-image' and 'maintaining a positive outlook', but at its core they advise people to *'accept that change is a part of living'*. By doing so, it keeps us alert to emerging change, and attentive to those small signs on the horizon. We may not be predicting the change, but we become lightning-quick at spotting it and have a mindset which keeps us nimble and able to adapt immediately to those changes.

Grit in the Oyster

"He who walks in another's tracks leaves no footprints." Joan Brannon

By definition, leaders are drawn both to do things in better ways or to do better things. In other words, they seek to change what is done and how we do it, and are a thorn in the side of those who wish to preserve the *status quo*. Leadership and change go hand-in-hand; to embrace leadership is to embrace change.

The moment you stand still, you start to fall behind, so constant progress is not an option; it's essential. Therefore, the best leaders routinely challenge themselves and their colleagues with searching questions such as: "How can we do this better?" or "What else can we do?" The core belief that what we have and what we do is 'not good enough' is surely the seed of all innovation; the catalyst for all innovative thought. Why would you ever look to improve and innovate, if you believed things *were* good enough?

So a leader's role cannot be solely about being reactive and adaptive to change. Whilst that openness is an essential first step, the best leaders also are proactive in initiating and shaping change, and encourage others to do likewise. These are the leaders who have a 'restless' mindset; they are the 'grit in the oyster'.

Innovation is all about the 'hard yards'

I remember so clearly a cartoon I watched as a kid, and I don't think I've ever been more on the edge of my seat. It featured a character who was a kind and hard-working family man, who also was exceptionally large and powerful, as only a cartoon character could be! His gift was that he could chop down trees at an incredible rate, so much so that this unassuming man had become the hero of his hometown (I guess the cartoon pre-dated today's environmental concerns!). One day an industrialist turned up with a mechanical device which, he claimed, could do the same task, but at an even faster rate. Impossible, surely? The gauntlet was thrown down, and during the next few minutes of the cartoon, as the chopping race unfolded, I was glued to the screen. All the locals had turned out to cheer on their mild-mannered hero, and I bet that every single kid watching was rooting for him too. Well, the two competitors ran neck and neck throughout the high speed competition, but just as the final bell rang, our hero faltered, and I'm devastated to tell you the machine triumphed! It was awful, and so unexpected! I sat in disbelief, crushed, as I watched the big hero being dispatched into retirement. How could a kid's cartoon end so cruelly? What on earth was the message that the producers were trying to send out?

Well, truth is, it was an *essential* message. New developments are a part of our everyday lives, and the scope to keep making improvements across all aspects of the world we live in only ever increases. Whilst the innate human desire for stability is within all of us, and the phrase 'comfort zone' is very appropriately named, we have to push our boundaries because, as T.S. Eliot put it, *"Only people who go too far find out how far you can go."*

The Wright brothers' quest to conquer powered-flight is a great example. The brothers famously endured countless failures and injuries as they borrowed a variety of spare parts from printing presses, bicycles and motors, before they finally succeeded in their quest on 17 December 1903. The brothers' engineering accomplishments to reach that point were remarkable, many remaining fundamentally unchanged in the aviation industry for decades. None were quick or easy to master, and many of the failures along the way were painful, literally! Persistence pays when it comes to innovation, with pretty much every successful product going through a long process of refinement to get it just right. For example, the everyday product 'WD-40' stands for 'Water Displacement 40th attempt' - straight out of the lab book used by Norm Larsen, the chemist who helped develop it back in 1953. Attempting to concoct a formula to prevent corrosion, which involves displacing water, Larsen's persistence paid off when he perfected the formula on his 40th try!

Big Steps, Small Steps

The Big Bang theory postulates that our universe came into being around 13.8 billion years ago, based amongst other things upon American astronomer Edwin Hubble's observation that the universe was expanding with galaxies drifting apart, and the further away they move the rate of expansion accelerates. The theory deduces therefore that 'in the beginning' our universe was extremely small, dense and hot, and that the initial expansion must have been explosively rapid. That was explosive change on an unimaginable scale.

When we look at the history of innovation it is tempting to view progress similarly, as a series of 'lightbulb' moments; just as Archimedes supposedly exclaimed *"eureka, eureka"* – meaning *'I have found (it)'* - as he noticed the water level rise upon immersing himself in his bath, thus instantly solving the problem of measuring the volume of irregular objects. Yet the reality of virtually all innovation is somewhat less dramatic or sudden. On being asked how he had 'discovered' the law or gravitation, Sir Isaac Newton replied: *"By thinking about it continually."* His discovery was many things, but it wasn't quick. Velcro and *Post-it* notes are both good examples of products that urban myth suggest were 'eureka' moments. Swiss engineer George de Mestral did indeed come up with the idea of Velcro from the sticky 'burrs' that clung to his trousers and his dog, but it took 14 years from his initial idea before Velcro was finally patented. *Post-it* notes are famed too for their rapid invention. However, it took the painstaking work and curiosity of engineer Spencer Silver to develop an extremely weak glue which most would consider useless, and the creative use of such a product by Arthur Fry, an engineer working for 3M, first on his church choir hymn book and then on reports that were circulated at 3M's offices for others' comments.

One current innovation entering our world is the material 'Graphene', formed from the carbon atom. Boasting some incredible properties such as being 200 times stronger than steel, incredibly lightweight, able to conduct electricity and so thin it is almost transparent, it is difficult to imagine the breadth of applications for this new 'wonder material'. However, it isn't actually new at all; indeed, around 60 years has passed since it was first identified. The challenge of 'isolating' it was cracked in 2004. Its researchers earned the 2010 Nobel Prize in Physics for it, and the scientists and investors began serious innovative use from 2012 onwards. It may appear to be 'new', but it's taken decades of perseverance to get it to the point of having practical applications.

So the message is: don't wait around for your 'bathtub' moment! Innovation takes a lot of thought and effort, often with small improvements emerging progressively over a long period of time. The process of rigorously identifying and implementing these gradual improvements, sometimes referred to as 'aggregate marginal gains' or '*kaizen*', is what has brought us most of the innovations we enjoy each day.

What is the answer to the question: "When is the best time to plant a tree?" Let's say the answer is: "20 years ago", reflecting the time it takes for that particular tree to mature and flourish. This long-term planning reflects the long-term process needed for most innovations. For many people though, such a long-haul can be daunting and demoralising. For those people the more important question would be: "When is the *second* best time to plant a tree?" The answer of course being: "Today!" Remember, when it comes to innovation, you have to encourage people to start those small steps, and start them *now*.

Many Ways to Innovate

There are contrasting views on the benefits of brainstorming, some researchers believing we innovate better when we are alone deep in our own thoughts, others suggesting the process of brainstorming is too structured or too hectic. Undoubtedly, there will be a case of 'each to his own', but after many years of incorporating brainstorming into our sessions, we are confident it is an effective process which has an important place in innovation.

There are many brainstorming techniques, so it is equally important to *vary* the approach and therefore the way you encourage others to innovate. At times, for example, a great approach can be to ask colleagues to visit other businesses and see what ideas they pick up, either to be adopted or adapted. At other times, there will be little better than an energetic team session with everyone firing in ideas as rapidly as they can and sparking off further ideas in each other. Yet, in contrast, quite often the key is to allow people to have uninterrupted time away from their working environment, for example strolling in a park or along a beach, to contemplate deeply. When it comes to encouraging innovation, don't be a 'one trick pony'.

However, on those occasions when you *do* want a collective process, try brainstorming but vary your technique. In our practice, we offer five alternatives that we have found very helpful:

Adapt: Key Question - *"How can we modify what we do, or what the product does, to improve or expand its use?"*

Our lives are deluged with such adaptations. Think about the cars we drive, constantly being adapted to include Bluetooth telephone connections, Sat Nav systems, heated seats, adjustable steering wheels, run-flat tyres, even Wi-Fi; the list goes on and on ... As a constant traveler, my gratitude goes to whoever came up with adding wheels to suitcases! And what about people living in remote or poor areas where batteries are unavailable or unaffordable? They can now enjoy the radio thanks to the addition of a wind-up handle to generate power.

Other Use: Key Question – *"What else could we do with this service or product?"*

If we think how many uses have been made of materials like Kevlar and carbon fibre, it is exciting to think of the applications for graphene, from the travel industry to military, construction, medicine and sport. In fact, it is harder to think of a field where it could not be applied. So, take an existing product, service or concept and brainstorm: "How could that be applied by us?"

Combine (1): Key Question – *"What different products and services can we incorporate to improve our offering?"*

Look no further than your mobile phone to illustrate the concept of *Combine*. Some of us are of an age where we can recall carrying a large briefcase with a mobile phone, a Filofax, a Walkman, a camera, the latest book and a pocket calculator all crammed in. Today, smartphones that slide into the slimmest pocket virtually run our lives. Opportunities to combine businesses are endless. Health food shops combine with personal trainers or sportswear, and car dealerships combine with insurance companies, who combine with advanced driving organisations.

Combine (2): Key Question – *"What can we learn from any other company or industry that we can blend with our business?"*

Imitation is 'the sincerest form of flattery', so what might you learn from others and apply to your business? For example, just as car dealerships allow people to test drive a car, many businesses that sell mattresses now adopt an equivalent practice. Disney have led the way at making queueing more pleasant or even entertaining, and their techniques are adopted all over the world in a myriad of businesses. Retailers learn from casinos by avoiding windows or clocks, keeping people engrossed and spending for longer. The options are endless, so get combining!

Eliminate: Key Question – *"What do we do that no longer adds value?"*

We spend too little time thinking about what we should *stop*! To make room for all our new ideas, we have to *stop doing* some things. Most teams we've worked with will quickly identify, for example, time-consuming reports they write that could be shortened, done less frequently or not written at all. Likewise, most people yearn for fewer, shorter and less frequent meetings! I personally find a hotel 'turn down' service to be completely unnecessary, even intrusive, and if I ran a hotel it would be the first thing eliminated!

Reverse: Key Question – *"How can we achieve the opposite of what we want?"*

This may seem a bizarre approach, but it's almost always great fun and surprisingly effective at producing great ideas. For example, if you want to brainstorm some great ideas to 'enhance customer experience', turn that goal around and task the group to think about: "What would really damage our customers' experience?" It seems odd at first, but encourage people to stick with it and come up with ideas like: "Let's hide from them," or "Let's make them queue for ages," or "Let's make them pay to come in," etc. Once you have a good range of suggestions, then reverse the task and ask "So, what would be the opposite of each of those suggestions?" For example, the opposite of 'hiding' is not simply being visible; it is 'approaching' your customers. So, instead of being a 'service assistant', upgrade to become a 'customer host'.

⚙ Action Point:

Make a point of encouraging your team into a more creative headspace. Particularly when engaging in *Combine* brainstorming, we suggest you introduce a simple yet energising activity such as 'Creative Pairs'. Allocate each person the name of an object. It can be absolutely anything from an abacus to a zebra. Then instruct the group to work in pairs to invent a new product using their two objects. Encourage the pairs to think of multiple options and to ignore practical considerations. Keep rotating the pairings every few minutes to keep the activity fresh. So, if a pair have a kitchenware company and a panda, then they might connect the black and white of a panda with salt and pepper and, therefore, decide to create panda-themed salt and pepper shakers. After 3-4 rotations, ask the group for their reactions and any ideas they liked. We encourage people to realise that innovation typically starts with an unrefined, perhaps even 'stupid', idea, but within that lies the seed of a great idea.

Dare to be Different

We all get stuck in our daily habits and working protocols, all of which are self-reinforcing. Sometimes it pays to just shake things up a little and try something new. It doesn't have to be perfect and most probably won't be, but people will experience something different, gain some new insights and, maybe, just maybe, become less stuck in their ways. Here are a few suggestions to get you started:

- Swap jobs with one of your colleagues for a day. Seriously, a 100% swap, and both agree to stand by any decisions the other makes.

- Don't use your car for a week. Use any other means of transport instead, particularly ones you would not normally use.

- Schedule a business meeting at 06.00, in an unusual location, make attendance 'optional', and see what unfolds.

- Serve the traditional courses of a meal in reverse.

- Do a random act of kindness; you choose the act and recipient, but be bold and make it meaningful.

- Invite for dinner someone you wouldn't normally invite.

With all these suggestions, and any others you think of, take time to reflect on what you experienced, what insights you gained, and what you and others learned from that.

⊛ Change Insights:

As we said at the start of this chapter, it is people who have an openness and willingness to embrace change that are most able to adapt and be successful in our fast-moving world. Encouraging such willingness often requires a little insight and inspiration so here is a selection that we've found helpful over the years:

Always keep one eye on the future: *"Chance favours the prepared mind."* (Louis Pasteur)

There is always a solution: *"We are continually faced by great opportunities brilliantly disguised as insoluble problems."*

Don't be put off by the scale of a task: *"All things are difficult before they are easy."* (John Norley)

At some point you have to jump in: *"Nothing will ever be attempted if all possible objections must first be overcome."* (Samuel Johnson)

Don't wait: *"If you plan to face tomorrow, do it soon."* (lyrics from 'Race among the Ruins' by Gordon Lightfoot)

Change requires learning, and that means you won't have all the capability today, but commit yourself to it, and you will succeed: *"The difference between successful people and others is not their strength, knowledge or skill, but rather their will."* (Vince Lombardi)

Change can leave you feeling out on a limb, but have the confidence to tough it out and lead the way: *"Never doubt that a small group of thoughtful, committed citizens can change the world; indeed, it's the only thing that ever has."* (Margaret Mead)

Don't expect all change to be in your favour. Stay adaptable and proactive, and it often is! Don't be the reactive person left feeling bitter: *"Resentment is like taking poison and waiting for the other man to die."* (Malachy McCourt)

Never allow yourself to adopt the 'victim' role: *"Destiny is not a matter of chance: it is a matter of choice - yours!"*

Expect that the planned change, will change, and **adapt as you go**: *"The pencil is mightier than the pen."* (Persig, in Lila)

Don't kid yourself or others **that it will be easy**, but do know that it'll be worth it: *"I find it fascinating that most people plan their vacations with better care than they plan their lives. Perhaps that is because escape is easier than change."* (Jim Rohn)

To conclude, the primary role of any change leader is to encourage people to **resist less and embrace more.** I'll leave it to Rod Stewart to endorse this, through his 'The Killing of Georgie' lyrics: *"Never wait or hesitate, get in kid before it's too late, for you may never get a second chance."* Rod was right; we need to move quicker, embrace risk more, tolerate occasional failure and emerge the other side perhaps at times feeling bruised, but always exhilarated and wiser for the experience.

I have facilitated many strategy sessions but have yet to advise anyone to take their company's funds to Las Vegas and head for the blackjack tables! Yet that is exactly what Frederick W. Smith, founder and CEO of FedEx, did when his company's funds were so depleted that they were unable to fuel their planes for the following week's deliveries. Having founded the company with a personal cash injection of $4m and raised an additional $90m in capital, just three years later Fred was staring at a bank balance of just $5,000.

Desperate times, as they say, call for desperate measures, and that certainly was true in Fred's case. He packed his bags and headed to the blackjack tables of the Las Vegas casinos, returning on the Monday morning with around $30,000, enough to keep the business afloat. Four decades later, with FedEx's market valuation standing at $60Bn, I think we can conclude Fred's gamble paid off!

Please don't draw the wrong conclusion here; I most definitely do not endorse a 'gambling' strategy. In any case, I think we can safely assume Fred, being extremely well-connected and from a wealthy background, would have had an easily-available 'Plan B'. Not all of us are so fortunate. Equally though, if we are not prepared to risk anything, how can we succeed? At some point, we have to back ourselves because ambition and progress can never be devoid of risk.

"Everybody dies. Not everybody lives." Tim Robbins (adapted)

The point of no return

In 49 BC Julius Caesar famously crossed the Rubicon river (well, actually, it was a small stream!) with a legion of his soldiers, declaring "alea iacta est", meaning 'the die is cast'. At that time, Governors of Roman provinces had the right to command their provinces, but legislation had drawn a line along the Rubicon, which marked the boundary into Rome that no Governor could cross with their army; to do so was to declare war on Rome. Caesar was initially heading to Rome by order of the Senate to stand trial on various charges, which historians mostly believe were trumped up to weaken his rapidly growing reputation. According to the historian Suetonius, Caesar was far from sure whether to 'come quietly' or to bring his soldiers with him, and he spent a sleepless night before deciding to cross. Ultimately, his decision was to cross the Rubicon with his legion and march on Rome, an act that would undoubtedly have meant the execution of Caesar and any soldier who followed him. However, so strong and fearsome was his reputation that as Caesar neared Rome, many of the Senate and military rulers fled rather than face him, paving his way to becoming Emperor.

We use the phrase 'crossing the Rubicon' today to signify those big decision points in life, when a person goes beyond 'the point of no return'. Caesar took a huge risk that day, literally risking his life and the lives of all his men, in taking that final step across the Rubicon. It is entirely natural and sensible to have doubts, but we can learn from Caesar's decision because most of our barriers to action can be symbolised by the Rubicon; it is fear that stops us crossing. That fear may be of failure, rejection, loss of employment or often just the uncertainty that entering 'new territory' brings. Yet these fears apply equally when we *do not* take risks. Indeed, it is said that in later life people regret far more the things they didn't do, than the things they did do. So, act or don't act, that is your choice, but whatever you decide, ask yourself:

• What are you stopping yourself from doing?

• Why won't you give it a go?

• What's the worst thing that could happen?

• What's the best thing that could happen?

• How will you feel if you do not take the risk?

• In a year's time what will you wish you had started today?

"There is only one way to avoid criticism: do nothing, say nothing, and be nothing." Aristotle

Pretty much everyone has an aversion to failure. It is natural to be that way, and it does to some extent protect us. After all, failure might bring the pain of lost income, damaged reputation, promotion opportunities washed away, a host of repercussions, colleagues telling you *"I told you so"*, embarrassment, frustration and anger. The list of undiluted misery is endless. Who in their right mind would sign up for all that!

The trouble is, fear of failure all too often grows in our heads and sucks the life-blood from us, preventing us from making progress. Yet, if you've never failed, you've never tried. We need a bit of fear; it is that very fear of failure that drives so many people towards success, to get things absolutely right first time and to care about not letting themselves and others down. It's about having fear in reasonable measure. Some risks are not smart, or at least are not handled in a smart way; you would neither test your parachute by jumping, nor test the depth of the water with both feet! As novelist Erica Jong put it: *"The trouble is, if you don't risk anything, you risk even more."* The courage required to take risks is well articulated by the Roman philosopher, Seneca: *"It is not because things are difficult that we do not dare; it is because we do not dare that things are difficult."*

"Behold the turtle. He only makes progress when he sticks his neck out." James Bryant Conant, President of Harvard University

Latest neuroscience points to the brain having a combination of 'excitatory' and 'inhibitory' cells. The former prompt us to try things out, to explore and, importantly, therefore to *learn*. The latter analyse the risks involved in a situation, encouraging us to hold back and, therefore, have a role in keeping us safe, but also stagnant. Evidence appears to show that younger brains have more activity going on amongst the excitatory cells and less amongst the inhibitory cells. Recognising this, as we move into adulthood we do have to make a conscious decision not to let our inhibitory cells hold us back too much. At some point, we have to find the courage to give things a go, to stand up and give it a try, accept the vulnerability of being a beginner who does not have all the answers and does not know for sure how a situation will work out. If you have never failed, the truth is you have never tried. Through all that, we must retain our humour and resilience when we fall flat on our face, secure in the knowledge that we are better for the experience, we have learned, and our day will come! Be ambitious for yourselves and for others; it is much easier to aim high and rein back a little than to aim low and try to gear up.

"If at first you do succeed, try something harder!" Ann Landers

Don't over-think it

Possibly the most intelligent member of the insect world is the bee, able for example to calculate distances more accurately than a computer, learn colours, and share information with hive members. Pretty smart, but that intelligence in some instances can work against them. If you entice a bee into a bottle and then place that bottle horizontally with the base against a window, the bee cannot escape because its intelligence leads it constantly towards the light outdoors; it makes no sense to fly away from the light. Yet, if you do the same with a common fly, strong candidate for 'most stupid' insect, it will fly erratically and randomly, and thus will eventually discover the 'illogical' narrow exit at the neck of the bottle.

We can all at times be a victim of our intelligence and experience, both of which can combine to convince us that we have found the 'one best way' of doing something. Whether that's the products we sell, the markets and customers we aim to serve, the delivery channels we utilise or the type of staff we seek, there always is the danger that we get set in our ways, convinced we are right, and all those 'set ways' discourage us from exploring new areas, and taking some risks.

Additionally, we are often dissuaded from taking risks by the power of our critical thinking. The ability to assess danger and risk is essential for survival, and our caring parents hone those skills in us throughout our childhood. Whilst some develop an appropriately cautious outlook which is to 'manage' risk to an acceptable level, for many others it's about 'eliminating' risk, an impossible goal and one that will hold you back so often. Sometimes you do just have to jump in, as author William Feather put it: *"Conditions are never just right. People who delay action until all factors are favorable do nothing."* Similarly, Samuel Johnson remarked: *"Nothing will ever be attempted if all possible objections must first be overcome."*

The message is simple; be careful not to over-analyse things. Sometimes you just have to explore a different path and see where it takes you. The final word, we'll leave to Theodore Roosevelt: *"Far better it is to dare mighty things, to win glorious triumphs, even though checkered by failure, than to take rank with those poor spirits who neither enjoy much nor suffer much, because they live in the gray twilight that knows not victory nor defeat."*

⊛ Risk Insights:

You are responsible for doing your own risk assessments; it is always your judgement call. However, I propose that too many people cross too few 'Rubicons', and they would benefit from sticking their necks out more.

Our fear of failure so often is exaggerated, and we *need* to fail at times, recognising the acronym FAIL stands for 'First Action In Learning'. None of us would ever had learned to walk without that attitude. Go on, 'up' your failure rate!!

Here are a few insights and quotes to prompt your thinking and discussions on risk-taking:

Courage is just a small step away: *"The difference between a hero and a coward is one step sideways."* (Gene Hackman)

Don't expect instant success; try, try and try again: *"Success is simply a matter of luck. Ask any failure."* Anon

No-one finds it easy, but find your inner strength and go for it: *"I'm a hero with coward's legs."* (Spike Milligan)

Don't worry: *"Worry does not empty tomorrow of its sorrow; it empties today of its strength."* (Corrie Ten Boom, concentration camp survivor)

Accept you can't have all the answers: *"Experience is something you don't get until just after you need it."*

Get over it(!): *"Whenever you make a mistake or get knocked down by life, don't look back at it too long. Mistakes are life's way of teaching you. Your capacity for occasional blunders is inseparable from your capacity to reach your goals. No one wins them all, and your failures, when they happen, are just part of your growth. Never quit, your turn will come."* (Og Mandino)

Be ambitious: *"If you know what to do to reach your goal, it's not a big enough goal."* (Bob Proctor)

If you point the finger of blame, three point back at you: *"Adulthood is defined by the willingness to accept full responsibility for where you are in life, no longer blaming others or circumstances."* (Joe Westbrook)

Choose your direction: *"One can choose to go back toward safety or forward toward growth. Growth must be chosen again and again; fear must be overcome again and again."* (Abraham Maslow)

Don't give up: *"It is inevitable that some defeat will enter even the most victorious life. The human spirit is never finished when it is defeated - it is finished when it surrenders."* (Prof Ben Stein)

Avoid a long boring life(!): *"Life is not a journey to the grave with the intention of arriving safely in a pretty and well preserved body, but rather to skid in sideways, thoroughly used up, totally worn out, and loudly proclaiming 'Wow, what a Ride!"* (Peter Sage)

'Safety' is an illusion: *"Security is mostly a superstition. It does not exist in nature nor do the children of man as a whole experience it. Avoiding danger is no safer in the long run than outright exposure. Life is either a daring adventure, or nothing."* (Helen Keller)

You've got to start somewhere, and accept that you won't always get it right: *"Good judgment comes from bad experience, and a lot of that comes from bad judgment."* (Anon)

Pushing our boundaries and exploring new territory liberates us from our static and comfortable worlds, and that exploration becomes addictive as we experience the joy of new encounters and realise how rarely we regret being curious and bold. Encourage your colleagues to look actively for new experiences, maybe prompting them with the question *"When was the last time you did something for the first time?"*

Find something, whether work or personal, that is new or stretching, and give it a go.

Positive Attitude

Do you see the pint glass as half-empty or half-full? It is a question that divides people. Some folk seem primed to appreciate and enjoy whatever they have in life, whilst others seem rooted in the disappointment of the things that they *don't* have and so focus upon what is lacking in their lives. I have met literally thousands of leaders over the past 20 years, and I haven't met a good one who was gloomy!

Given that the purpose of leadership is to instil enthusiasm towards higher achievements and new directions, it makes sense that a 'can do' spirit will pay dividends. As sales coach Jeffrey Gitomer puts it: *"Obstacles can't stop you. Problems can't stop you. Most of all, other people can't stop you. Only you can stop you."*

Few people epitomise 'positive spirit' more than Alessandro 'Alex' Zanardi. Born in Italy in 1966, Zanardi showed great determination to compete in karting, even building his own kart, aged 13, from spare parts. He went on to compete in both the Formula 3 and 3000 series, and entered the world of Formula 1 in 1991. Perhaps most notable was Zanardi's tenacity in securing a 'drive' with various teams across different competitions and embracing every challenge.

In 2001 his tenacity though would become tested in far more dramatic circumstances. Competing at the EuroSpeedway Lausitz race track, a unique oval shaped track in Europe which allows for average speeds of around 250km/h, Zanardi was leading the race and making his last pit stop. Accelerating back out, his attempt to merge back onto the track came to a disastrous end as he collided at speed with another car. The huge impact severed the nose of Zanardi's car, along with his legs. Medical teams worked to save his life and as much as they could of his legs, but one was amputated at the thigh and the other at the knee. For most people that would spell the end to their racing career, but not for Zanardi. He continued to compete using adapted cars and incredibly went on to win the 2005 World Touring Car Championship. A brief revisit to F1 testing in 2006 made Zanardi realise that having to use his left hand to operate the throttle, and steer with just his right hand was impossible to do competitively.

However, the greatest measure of Zanardi's tenacity and positive spirit came elsewhere. In 2007, he discovered a way to compete on a level playing field, through the sport of Handcycling. His iron-will continued to feature as prominently as ever, and he has gone on to win four Olympic Gold medals and eight World Championship Gold medals. Perhaps his remarkable spirit shone even brighter when he competed in the 2014 Ironman World Championship; using a handbike for the cycling section and a wheelchair for the running section, he came 19th out of 247 athletes in his age category. Zanardi comments: "I've always tried to see the glass half-full. Everything I now do is related to my new condition, and I have a great life. So you'd have to say losing my legs was one of the greatest opportunities of my life."

Alex Zanardi provides a great example of Henry Ford's assertion: *"If you think you can, or think you can't, you're probably right."* His irrepressible spirit is an inspiration to us all. In this section, we look at various factors that support us having a positive outlook.

Be Happy

"We either make ourselves happy or miserable. The amount of work is the same." Carlos Castaneda

Around 2,500 years ago, there lived a kind-hearted young prince named Siddhartha Gautama, who was deeply troubled by the poverty and suffering he so regularly encountered on his travels. Aged just twenty-nine, Gautama set off on a personal quest to understand what lay behind all this suffering. After many years of counselling elders and meditating, he reached a simple conclusion; we suffer because we always desire more. And this constant craving leads to constant dissatisfaction and the myriad of negative emotions and behaviours that stem from that. The goal of escaping these negative effects, became known as 'nirvana', meaning 'extinguishing the fire', and the route to achieve this was to learn to appreciate the moment, to enjoy the 'now'. Gautama is known today as Buddha, meaning 'the enlightened one', and Buddhists encourage us to realise that 'the only happiness is now', by which they mean you cannot feel happiness yesterday, or tomorrow; you can only feel it 'now'.

Our happiness depends far less on what we have, and far more on how we feel about what we have. A car enthusiast friend of mine once commented how rarely he had seen drivers of a particular supercar brand actually smiling. 'Surely not,' I thought. That car company produces some of the most beautiful cars on the planet; they must be awesome to drive. I started paying attention to his observation, and I have to say he does seem to be right. Whilst that's rather depressing, it does at least mean I can stop yearning for my first supercar to finally make me happy! We can be happy with little, yet miserable with much. Indeed, studies into the correlation between general happiness levels and income levels follow a classic bell-curve i.e. happiness rises as people's incomes rise, but there comes a point when it plateaus (this currently seems to be around £70,000 p.a.), beyond which the correlation inverts i.e. as income continues to grow, happiness levels actually decline. Success, it seems, is not the key to achieving happiness. Conversely, it is rather more likely that happiness is the key to achieving success! In the workplace there seems to be an innate concern that happiness, or fun, equals frivolity or lack of focus. Rarely is that true. Instead, it brings a real 'buzz', which is one of the best intangible assets to have on your balance sheet. The author Grenville Kleiser recognized this around a century ago, pointing out: *"Good humor is a tonic for mind and body. It is the best antidote for anxiety and depression. It is a business asset. It attracts and keeps friends. It lightens human burdens, and is the direct route to serenity and contentment."*

"He who laughs, lasts." Mary Pettibone Poole

The connection between humour and health is irrefutable, medical research showing that laughter lowers the pulse rate while increasing oxygen flow to muscles. It produces endorphins which directly improve our mood and reduce our stress, and protects and defends us too, by increasing the number of Immunogloblin A antibodies in our immune system, making us stronger. The ability to put our cares and worries aside and enjoy the moment is so critical in life, and a hallmark of positive leadership. Yet, evidence that young children laugh on average 150 times a day, whilst adults laugh on average just 5 times a day, is enough to make you depressed! But at least recognising this, we can look to appreciate the lighter side of life more frequently, and encourage others to do likewise. So, come on leaders, bring a bit of fun to the workplace, let the sun shine in; it's good for the spirit, the body *and* the business!

"To succeed in life you need three things; a wishbone, a backbone, and a funny bone." Reba McEntire

Some people's ability to stay happy and positive, despite the worst adversity is simply inspiring. BBC journalist Helen Fawkes wrote an upbeat and inspiring blog throughout her fight with ovarian cancer. Diagnosed at age 30, sadly she eventually died at the age of 44, but not before she had done so much to live her life to the full and inspire so many around her. Her blog entry: "I'm not terminally ill, but I will die a lot sooner than I ever imagined" summed up her pragmatic and positive view on life.

Philanthropy vs Fun

The work of Professor Martin Seligman has helped identify where people derive happiness from. He concludes there are three principal sources. The first is through leading a *pleasant life*, enjoying the day-to-day activities that bring us immediate pleasure, whether that's country walks, listening to music, playing sport etc. It is an important component of our happiness, but the evidence is that such activities bring momentary, rather than lasting, happiness. The second source is through leading a *good life*, enjoying inter-personal engagement with people we are close to and care about, and also having fulfilling work. These factors lead to a deeper and more enduring sense of happiness. The third source, which consistently results in the deepest and most enduring feelings of happiness, is what he called the *meaningful life*. By this he means altruistic devotion to a 'cause', something that is bigger than us, that we can contribute to and make the world a better place. Whether this is a religion, the environment, our communities, or helping individuals less fortunate than us, all the evidence points to this type of activity correlating strongly with long-term happiness.

Seligman created an activity he called 'Philanthropy versus Fun' to prove the point. His students were asked to engage in one 'pleasurable' activity (say, playing a computer game) and one 'philanthropic' activity (say, helping a person with special needs), and then to write about both. What he discovered was that the philanthropic activities had a far greater positive impact on his students, creating a much deeper and lasting sense of fulfilment and self-worth. Happiness it seems is rooted in thinking about yourself less, and about others more.

"If you want others to be happy, practice compassion. If you want to be happy, practice compassion." Dalai Lama

There are few better business examples than Timpson, a family-owned national chain of high street key-cutters and shoe repairers in the UK. John and Alex Timpson had three children, adopted another two, and went on to foster more than 90 children over a 30-year period. They have various charitable foundations, and in their business have an active policy of hiring ex-offenders to give them a fresh chance in life, with an outstandingly high success rate. Notable too is how little publicity they seek for any of their remarkable work; they do it because it's good behaviour, not because it's good PR. I walked past a local outlet recently, and there was an advert outside offering free dry cleaning to anyone unemployed who needed smart clothes for an interview. The Timpson outlets are an ever-present feature on our High Streets, with the strapline under the shop name reading 'Great Service by Great People'. We applaud you Timpson, and long may your success last.

There is a rather clichéd saying about how you can't get rid of love because 'however much love you give, more keeps coming back'; the same it would appear is true for happiness!

In It for Others

"People with humility don't think less of themselves, they just think about themselves less." Norman Vincent Peale

Ralph Nader proposed: *"The function of leadership is to produce more leaders, not more followers,"* and I have encountered many leaders who selflessly mentored their colleagues to be their successors, with that being an entirely positive outcome for both parties. Being 'in it for others' makes sense from many perspectives. It draws the best people towards you; let's face it, you represent a good proposition for them! It also makes no sense for you to be irreplaceable; if you can't be replaced, you can't be promoted. No-one is fooled by the airbrushed image of the unassailable leader anyway, but the good news is, just as people are turned off by unconvincing images of perfection, being 'normal' is rather appealing. Such normality means people can more confidently aspire to reach your level.

So, be visible and accessible, and above all be 'real'. Genghis Khan was both ruthless and much-feared, yet wrote of his concerns about his prize warrior Yessutai: *"No man alive is braver than Yessutai, no march can tire him; he feels neither hunger nor thirst. That is why he is totally unfit to command."* Even Genghis understood the need for a healthy 'connection' message, increasingly relevant in today's world where we see the gradual dismantling of life's hierarchical systems. People are less inclined to look up to others purely because of their status. Likewise, it doesn't matter how great you are, you have to recognise that you're merely a cog in the machine, however big that cog may be. Imagine how dominant a player basketball legend Michael Jordan must have been as a child, playing in the parks and amateur ranks. Yet, he revealed one of the best pieces of advice he had received from a junior team coach: *"Michael, you can't play if you can't pass."* None of us can play, if we don't learn to 'pass'.

History is littered with examples of leaders who were not in it for their 'team'. When the Duke of Wellington enlisted in the British army aged just eighteen, as part of the upper class 'elite' he was immediately commissioned as an officer. It would appear he thought very little of the low-ranking soldiers under his command, writing to a fellow aristocrat: *"We have in the service the scum of the earth as common soldiers."* It is hard to imagine he did anything to improve the conditions of his people, and even less likely that he formed any personal connection with them. His only influence will have been founded on power, not respect. Similarly, the Chinese bureaucrats who ruled the ancient armies looked down with disdain upon those who carried the swords as disposable resources, and did not allow anyone of any social standing to join their ranks, epitomised by their saying: *"Do not waste good iron to make nails."*

However, in today's leadership world none of that will wash. Treat people like cannon fodder and performance will plummet, and the best folk will walk away. Showing that you care about people and being considerate aren't differentiators, they're leadership essentials.

"Be like the bamboo, the higher you grow the deeper you bow."
Chinese proverb

Stephen King's short story *Last Rung on the Ladder* concerns the tale of a brother and sister whose relationship loses its way in adult life, although their childhood relationship was full of hope and inspiration. The siblings had been playing in their family's barn, taking turns to climb to the top of a ladder, when the ladder suddenly broke leaving the sister clinging precariously to the very last rung. In desperation, the brother piled hay beneath her as quickly as he could, and when she clearly could no longer hold her grip he shouted for her to let go. The hay broke her fall and saved her from serious injury. What amazed the brother was when she told him that she hadn't looked down before letting go, and had not seen the pile of hay. She had simply trusted him to save her. Building amongst others this sort of innate belief that you would do all you reasonably could to help them is a benchmark for a great leader.

Leaders who have their colleagues' interests at heart in this way, who care about them and support them, build enormous levels of trust, and in exchange they earn the rewards of loyalty and commitment. Thankfully, leaders today more than ever recognise that getting people to like you is simply the other side of liking other people. Creating an atmosphere of equality and respect pays dividends in today's world. Stefan Edberg is an outstanding example; despite being ranked World No.1 tennis player, winning seven Grand Slam titles, including Wimbledon twice, he always treated every single person on the circuit with the utmost respect. He explained his personal philosophy: *"Everyone's important, and no-one's very important."* It is no surprise he was, and remains, one of the most admired personalities within the sport.

"After the game, the king and the pawn go into the same box."
Italian proverb

Let's leave the final word to Arsenal and England soccer captain Tony Adams, a much-admired player who always put team ahead of individuals, including himself. His outlook on life was encapsulated perfectly by his ethos: *"Play for the name on the front of the shirt, and they'll remember the name on the back."* Do you play for the team, or for yourself?

The Big Five

Our personalities form the core of *who we are*, and there is broad agreement that our personalities comprise five broad components, known as the 'Big Five': *Openness to Experience, Extraversion -v- Introversion, Emotional Stability, Agreeableness and Conscientiousness.*

Being somewhat intangible, they are difficult to research with precision and certainty. However, there is strong consensus amongst psychologists that our personalities develop from a combination of our DNA and our experiences i.e. from *nature* and *nurture* and that the majority of this development takes place very early on in life, as young as 2-3 years old. Conventional wisdom holds that personality does continue to develop, albeit to a lesser extent into adolescence, and beyond that it is largely set.

Emerging research has started to indicate that some of the 'Big Five' do in fact continue to be moulded by later life experiences.

However, let's not debate to what extent people's personalities shift over time because that is not the key concern here. That is because, whilst personalities clearly influence behaviours, we all nonetheless remain in complete control of how we act. For example, 'Openness to experience' refers to a person's preference for new experiences versus more consistent experiences in familiar territory, and that trait clearly will influence, say, a person's holiday choice. The former will tend towards opting to experience a new destination each time, with the latter preferring to return to her familiar holiday haven. However, both have complete control over their actions, and could easily decide to do the opposite of their preference. What is key is that both personality types become aware of their innate preference and develop the ability to consider alternative options. The same is true for all five factors, and so your personality should be seen as a 'grow bag' not a 'coffin'; make the most of it, and learn to adapt where it's helpful to do so.

The personality factors tend to be expressed in terms of 'preferences' rather than 'strengths and weaknesses' because there are pros and cons to each preference. You may think, for example, that you'd like all your recruits to score high on *openness to experience* so they adapt quickly to changes and even stimulate change themselves, yet you may well find the stability, perseverance and loyalty of someone who scored low on that scale to be just as attractive or necessary. That said, two of the five have a rather clearer link to 'strengths and weaknesses' and are particularly relevant in the context of leaders having a positive attitude:

- *'Agreeableness'* refers to the extent to which a person is easy to rub along with and is amiable and likeable. Evidence clearly points to such people enjoying success far more commonly, across all aspects of their personal and professional life. That is no surprise, as their comparatively high orientation towards others is an attractive trait, which draws people towards them. After all, liking others is just the other half of being liked, so when recruiting your leaders, undervalue this personality trait at your peril!

- *'Emotional stability'* influences how well we deal with difficult situations. Those with a 'high' score experience more stress and anxiety, which lead to various negative emotions such as anger or upset and, consequently, to less helpful behaviours towards others. 'Low' scorers, on the other hand, take things more in their stride and as a result deal with negative situations with fortitude and even humour. They are able to maintain a sense of perspective, perhaps underpinned by H.G.

Wells' advice: *"The crisis of today is the joke of tomorrow."* This ability reduces not only their own stress but also the stress of those around them.

Keep it Real

There is a cautionary note to all this positivity, which is explored superbly by Barbara Ehrenreich in her book *Smile or Die,* in which she challenges the common belief that remaining ever-positive is the route to success. Sure, it is good to be around people who see the pint glass as half full and, conversely, those who tend to see it as half empty can be a drag, but if our positivity extends to insisting that everything will always work out well, if we just believe in that, we're simply denying the reality of life. Whilst we tend to say 'ignorance is bliss', let's face it sometimes life sucks, and we are confronted by a problem that we could not have predicted. To blindly insist everything is fine leads us to ignore signs of danger and restricts our ability to take appropriate action.

Alex Honnold is without doubt a serious risk-taker. As one of the world's foremost 'free' climbers, i.e. using no ropes or safety devices, he has earned countless accolades for his remarkable climbs, such as first ever 'free solo' climb of Yosemite's 'El Capitan'. It's just Honnold versus the rock face. To most of us, what he does seems insanely dangerous; you rarely get a second chance in that sport, and many participants have died pursuing their passion. Despite intense training to attain his phenomenal strength and fitness levels, and clearly possessing a cold and calculating mind, Honnold is, however, never blasé. Far from mentally blocking out the dangers, he describes his approach to risk: "I visualise the worst, to keep myself honest. If you only visualise the best, you'll sucker yourself into something you're not ready for." He stresses that there is nothing wrong with being afraid and that 'fear' is telling you something, so use it to make informed decisions.

In the business world, the phrase 'burning platform' is used in the context of leading change. When there *is* a crisis, it would rarely make sense to hide it, and so ensuring people are 'appropriately' alarmed is fully justified. Similarly, in less dramatic circumstances, people who face reality head-on are better able to assess and respond to challenging situations. In similar vein, but from a more positive perspective, if leaders can offer an 'irresistible vision' then people will embrace the change that comes with it. Either way, if we deny the reality of life and the opportunities that lie waiting for us, we live in a state of mistaken or deluded happiness, and skip along carelessly through life. The fact is that sometimes life throws curved balls at us and demands that we think more deeply about what's around us, and make some critical and uncomfortable assessments. We can make much progress in those sober and serious moments.

"When you are happy, you enjoy the music. When you are sad, you understand the lyrics." Anon

This whole cautionary point is also relevant in our section on Authenticity in Chapter 13. People who are positive 24/7 simply come across as fake; nobody's life and prospects are *that* enduringly fantastic. If we want to connect well with others we have to be prepared to show our real selves; openness and honesty about concerns and vulnerabilities are well-established contributors to the forming of deep relationships.

The Final Word: Let's not finish the subject of being positive on a negative because positivity pays dividends 99% of the time! Leaders and high performers undoubtedly embrace their positive sides far more frequently than others and that, unquestionably, beis part of their recipe for success. Because 'attitudes are infectious', their positivity spreads to everyone willing to catch it. Steven Spielberg once divulged: *"I wake up so excited, I can't eat breakfast."* Imagine working with a team of Spielbergs!

Positive Attitude

Continual Improvement 7

I mentioned earlier the Wright brothers' remarkable achievement in conquering the challenge of controlled powered flight and how their quest, and eventual success, had little to do with 'eureka' moments.

Despite having extremely limited funding compared to others who were competing to master the challenge, Wilbur and Orville showed remarkable tenacity in a constant cycle of innovate-test-innovate-test etc. to achieve their goal.

It was this relentless pursuit of marginal improvements that eventually combined to earn them their place in history.

A dedication to continual improvement lies behind pretty much every success story we will ever encounter.

Few sports illustrate obsession with marginal gains more clearly than F1 Motorsport, where winning margins in the 305km long Grand Prix's can boil down to fractions of seconds. With such tiny margins determining the race outcome, optimising the performance of the entire team, not just the driver, is paramount. Critical amongst the team are the pit stop mechanics, whose performance can make or break the driver's chances of winning. Around 2010, the best pit stops were timed at about 4 seconds, not bad considering all four wheels are changed and any other mechanical adjustments made. Only three years later, the Red Bull pit stop team broke the world record at the US Grand Prix, with an incredible time of 1.92 seconds. It is scarcely believable, and shows what happens when people become obsessed with marginal gains.

Equally fascinating is the story of the Williams pit stop team. They had had a miserable 2015 season, plagued by errors and problems that had cost their results dearly. It was precisely this 'failure' that led the team to step back and look afresh at every single component of what they did. Breaking down the entire pit stop process, analysing all the mechanical aspects involved at each stage, and even addressing 'human' factors such as introducing a physio to work with the crew, enabled the Williams team to transform their performances. By the following season, the Williams crew were the standout pit stop performers, achieving the fastest time in 14 of the 21 races, including equaling Red Bull's record time of 1.92 seconds at the 2016 Azerbaijan Grand Prix. Commentators within the sport report that several teams are aiming to bring times down to 1.7 seconds. Now, that's continuous improvement!

There are few leadership responsibilities more important than encouraging others to continually develop. Senator Bill Bradley, a former professional basketball player, had a great approach to continual improvement. His mantra was: *"When you are not practising, remember, someone somewhere is, and when you meet him he will win."* The field of sport gives us many insights into elite performance, but what always stands out is the person's willingness to try, try, and try again. The impact of this attribute goes way beyond the world of sport. In fact, American

Football coach Vince Lombardi put it: *"The quality of a person's life is in direct proportion to their commitment to excellence, regardless of their chosen field of endeavor."* There are so few exceptions to this, and so as leaders we have to find ways to encourage people to believe in themselves, to give things a try, and to keep going even when the results aren't great. As Mark Twain said: *"Keep away from small people who try to belittle your ambitions. Small people always do that. But the really great make you feel that you too can become great."*

"Nobody made a greater mistake than he who did nothing because he could only do a little." Edmund Burke

Turning to the workplace, new technologies and ongoing change are forcing an unprecedented rate of learning upon those who strive to be employable, both in existing jobs and in jobs that are yet to emerge in our ever-changing world. Traditional cradle-to-grave employment has been consigned to the history books. Today's generations face decreasing levels of job security and employment longevity, and we should not be surprised or critical when they respond with higher self-orientation and lower loyalty. Evidence clearly points to today's employees focusing as much on being employable as they do on being employed. Yes, the latter pays the bills, and we all have some need for security, but few can ignore the perils of allowing their employability to erode. As industrialist Harold Geneen said: *"In the business world, everyone is paid in two coins: cash and experience. Take the experience first; the cash will come later."*

If we only knew how much capability lay within us, we might be scared and daunted, or maybe just plain excited. As Neuro-linguistic Programming co-founder John Grinder quipped: *"If the brain was so simple that we could understand it, we would be so simple that we couldn't."* Our brains have immense capacity, much of it lying unused, so whether you're driven by success or by survival, these days your willingness and ability to learn will determine how your life plays out. Increasingly people 'get' this; the recruitment firm Manpower reported in 2017 that '93% of young people want ongoing skills development, and four out of five say the opportunity to learn a new skill is a top factor when considering a new job'. Similarly, the survey company Q&R report that the second most important factor leading to workplace happiness is 'intellectual challenge' (the first was 'feeling valued and supported', and more about that later in this section), which provides further evidence that employees do want to be stretched and in doing so they will grow, as will their employability. The physician Oliver Wendell Holmes observed well over a century ago that *"Man's mind, once stretched by a new idea, never regains its original dimensions"*. Whilst stretch is far from a new concept, what has changed is how this 'stretch' has shifted from being the exclusive preserve of highly successful people, to being essential to *everyone*. Stretch is as relevant to survival as it is to success; so we all must stretch!

The 'lifelong learning' graph below shows just how radically the nature and goal of learning has changed over just one generation:

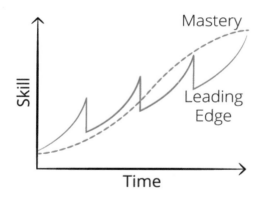

The dotted-curved line reflects what previous generations will instantly recognise as a traditional career-learning process. In brief, we started by being inducted and may well have had very few immediate learning opportunities, but as we progressed, our learning accelerated to reflect our growing commitment, reputation and contribution. Eventually, that learning flattened off as we established ourselves as 'masters of our trade'. At that point, the need to learn reduced significantly, and instead we merely reaped the rewards of our lifetime's efforts and, in addition, hopefully were sufficiently benevolent to pass on our knowledge and skills to those following in our steps.

However, in today's world, a typical learning journey is represented far more accurately by the solid-wavy line. Modern careers are considerably more varied and turbulent, with the average time in a single job currently standing at just over 4 years (ref US Bureau of Labor Statistics), and it is further estimated that a third of the skills required by workers will change every 3-4 years. This results in four notable differences:

- First, the wavy lines are almost exclusively steeper than the curved line, which means we must learn more, and faster.

- Secondly, there are more 'waves', reflecting the fact that our learning covers a broader range of topics, and new subjects constantly arise.

- Thirdly, each 'wave' is followed by regular vertical downwards lines, reflecting the many times when our existing knowledge becomes outdated and redundant, and we need to 'unlearn' it and move on.

- Fourthly, the end goal is no longer 'mastery'; that simply doesn't exist anymore. Instead, the goal today is to keep at the 'leading edge'.

I encountered a great example of this a few years back working with a group of medical consultants. Their intellect, capability and professionalism stood out a mile, yet what impressed me most was how none of them considered themselves 'masters'. They no doubt present a reassuring image of calm omniscience when they are with their patients but, just like the swan, they are peddling fast below the surface to keep abreast of the relentless and exciting progress in their chosen field. In politics we have recently seen a 70-year-old US President candidate, and victor, embrace social media to avoid the 'lens' of the media. Political views aside, you have to acknowledge that that was smart learning and adaptation. The same is true for all of us; lifelong learning will drive both our success and survival.

"One hour per day of study will put you at the top of your field within three years. Within five years you'll be a national authority. In seven years, you can be one of the best people in the world at what you do." Earl Nightingale

The benefits of lifelong learning extend way beyond enhancing our careers. It is proven also to improve our earning power, our friendships and our health. The danger though is that we see 'education' as something that we engage in during our school and college days; and beyond that we stop learning and 'get on with our jobs'. Doing that leaves us 'academically pigeon-holed' as very young adults. A senior member of Oxford University staff is quoted: *"If at first you don't succeed, you don't succeed"* and I have no doubt there is a significant truth to that. Those who flourish through their formative years tend to go on to do so in their adult lives also, and sadly *vice versa*. However, it simply does not have to be that way, and the best leaders do not see it that way either. They recognise the potential in everyone, at whatever stage in life they are, and never stop encouraging, cajoling and even pressurising their colleagues into learning. It can be hard work, and not everyone will thank you for it at the time, but at some point your colleagues will come to realise how lucky they were to have such as 'enabling' leader as you!

Action Point:

Make it part of your repertoire to ask colleagues questions such as "What have you learned this week?"; "What have you learned from this project?"; "What have you struggled with that you could try to improve upon?" or "What sorts of things would you like to develop?" Just showing this interest will itself set you apart as a good leader and will inspire people to focus on their development and employability. If you then step up to enquire: "And how can I support that learning?" your leadership goes from 'good' to 'great'.

Diagnosing Performance Issues

When it comes to supporting someone's development it's essential to diagnose *why* they perform at the level they do. It is overly-simplistic to say someone is 'good' or 'bad' at something because there are so many factors that affect performance. We use the model below to help us consider the aspects at stake:

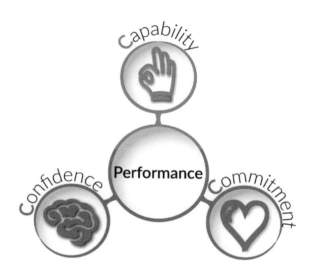

1. **Capability** ... is the easiest component to diagnose. Simply, do they have the knowledge and skills necessary to achieve the task? Their level of knowledge and skill can, in most cases, be objectively assessed, and any gaps or opportunities to dial-up capability levels can be identified and remedied. As a result, conversations regarding this aspect of performance are generally objective and straightforward, and because most people today have embraced lifelong learning, they are receptive and appreciative of opportunities to develop their skills.

2. **Confidence** ... is a more-subtle and often covert issue, and it can take time and emotional intelligence to get the issue on the table. There are so many reasons why a person's confidence may have taken a hit. This should not be ignored because the world is

full of people who have both the capability and desire to achieve something, yet an 'invisible barrier' holds them back. Take a look at the following 'confidence crunchers', and see which you have encountered, either personally or in relation to someone you know:

a. Limiting self-belief. We have all heard and said many of the following comments: "I was never any good at … *insert an infinite number of competencies, such as maths, music, presenting, sport, sociability, time management etc." They will go on to tell you: "Even my teachers said I wouldn't excel in that area"; "My sister was such a natural at that, I could never be like her" or "My last boss never trusted me in that area." There are very few comments that provide greater opportunity for a leader to help people re-appraise their confidence, because rarely are they true.

Challenge people who make comments like those, in a friendly and supportive manner, and encourage them with any feedback you have to dispute their low self-opinion. Encourage them to embrace, rather than avoid, the area they should develop. It is ironic that we label these as issues of *self-belief,* yet they almost inevitably stem from what others have said to us so they are in fact *others'-belief.* As a leader, be the person who challenges and reverses those prejudices and helps people towards a more positive self-belief.

b. Previous bad experience. You've also heard many comments such as: "I've tried that before and it went horribly wrong!" or "Life's too short to play to your weaknesses." Whilst I do have some sympathy with the latter comment, in that it does make a lot of sense to play most of the time to your strengths and preferences, you nonetheless must explore the reality of their bad experience before accepting such comments. Do they have a wildly exaggerated sense of how bad their previous experience was? An effective technique is to ask people to explain *specifically* why their experience was so bad because *specifics* force the brain to be objective, and therefore see their exaggerated thinking. If they make a presentation and report back: "Most of the audience were bored stiff," then ask them:

"How, *specifically*, do you know that?" Very rarely will they say: "28 people fell asleep," or "the feedback comments all said it was boring." Instead, whilst it may not have been the most exhilarating speech, an objective review allows them to see the reality of the situation. Additionally, it allows them to consider wider contributory factors, for example perhaps the subject matter was dry, the room was too warm, the audience weren't quite appropriate for the content, or theirs was the fourth presentation in a row, and people simply needed a break. Whatever the case happened to be, the best leaders ask "So, what did you learn from that experience that would enable you to make a more engaging presentation next time?"

c. Perfectionism. The field of psychology called Transactional Analysis identifies five 'Drivers' that subconsciously influence what we do, and how we do it. One of those Drivers, known as 'Be Perfect', is particularly relevant here. Those with a *Be Perfect* driver place enormous value on correctness and precision. As such, they will avoid any situation where they might make mistakes or be open to criticism. *Be Perfects* work so hard to present a perfect image that it becomes part of their identity, and so they become ever-more unlikely to risk jeopordising that. As a leader, whilst acknowledging their dedication to perform with precision, you must also encourage them out of their safe environment.

As racing driver Mario Andretti put it: *"If everything's under control, you're not going fast enough."* Sometimes, those who get furthest in life achieve that by getting closer to the edge, incurring a few scratches and hitting a few bumps in the road. Setting high standards is admirable and very often the foundation for success, but there's a line beyond which it can become inefficient - when the 'Law of Diminishing Returns' proves their precision to be disproportionate to the benefits achieved. Returning to the pit stop crews we discussed at the start of this chapter, many of the racing teams are making rational decisions about how much more they want to invest in trying to shave hundredths of seconds off an event that happens two or three times a race, when a similar investment could perhaps shave that amount of time off every single lap. In a business context, I have a major client whose employees are extremely professional and capable, but recognising some of the pitfalls of their culture of perfectionism, the organization has adopted the phrase: "Don't let *great* get in the way of *good.*" It is not intended to infer that "mediocre is OK", rather to encourage a sense of practicality and balance.

d. Fear of failure. The saying: "Nothing fails like success" warns against the perils of complacency. Similarly, in his book *Black Box Thinking*, Matthew Syed comments: "This is the paradox of success: it is built upon failure." The only way we can ever improve is to give it a go and accept the failures that come with it and to learn from those experiences, persevering until we have mastered the skill. Therefore, 'failure' comes before 'success' in both the dictionary and in life! Notwithstanding this critical role that failure plays, or *should* play, in our lives, the reality is most of us avoid it at all costs. You hear examples of 'failure avoidance' all the time, in comments like: "If I mess this up, we'll lose the contract"; "If it doesn't work, it'll damage my reputation" or "I wouldn't be able to handle that role, because no-one would respect my position." Comments like these reflect a fear of negative outcomes that the person does not feel equipped to handle. There is some justification for those fears when the person has built no strategies for dealing with the inevitable occasions when things do not go to plan. To tackle this, leaders can pursue two valuable lines of enquiry. First, simply ask: "Honestly, what's the worst that can happen?" This conversation itself can go a long way to help them see objectively that their fears have become magnified or irrational. Secondly, asking: "What strategies can you develop to deal with such a situation, should it arise?" enables people to prepare for the challenging situation, reassured that they have a contingency plan should their fears become reality.

e. Unfavourable comparisons. Everything in life is relative, so it can be difficult when you are surrounded by high performers. It's easy to see why some people can conclude that it is better for team members to rigidly play to their strengths, in other words to 'let the expert do it'. But that's a short-term strategy, where no-one grows. Yet leaders can turn this constraint into a huge opportunity by praising high-performers for their competence, whilst at the same time enlisting their support in up-skilling colleagues, even targeting and rewarding them for doing so. At the same time, help the learners see that you are impressed by an appetite to learn, which encourages people to be 'beginners', and jump straight in to embrace new experiences.

⊛ Action Point:

Share the above list with colleagues who you feel may benefit from addressing their confidence levels. The discussion will raise their self-awareness, and also should enable them to focus on how best to raise their confidence.

3. **Commitment** … is relatively easy to diagnose, because it is almost always overt and on display. The word 'motivation' derives from the Latin *motus*, which means 'to move', and movement is plain to see. Motivated people arrive early, are well -prepared, go the extra mile, ask for feedback and act on it, care when things go wrong, and are excited when things go right. Whilst the unmotivated lounge around, motivated people are always 'on the go'; for them, *"Well done"* is better than *"Well said"*. What's more, these people spread their motivation, because 'attitudes are infectious', and 'behaviour breeds behaviour'.

However, whilst it is relatively easy to assess levels of commitment, what can prove more difficult is diagnosing *why* there is a commitment issue, and how that can be addressed. You should, at least, have the conversation and explore to what extent they are 'intrinsically' and 'extrinsically' motivated, as discussed below:

a. Intrinsic Motivation. **Why** do you do what you do? In other words, what meaning does this have for you? This conversation explores a person's 'intrinsic' motivators, and whilst it's a conversation few leaders even think of entering into, it is a critical one because intrinsic motivators are invariably powerful and enduring. This relates closely to the section on 'Inspirational' leadership in Chapter 1, where leaders are able to understand and engage with people's personal values i.e. the things that are most important to them. We gave the example of the hotel receptionist, explaining how the 'higher purpose' for every job presents the biggest opportunity to inspire true commitment. Similarly, a florist may be drawn to his job because the location is convenient, or the pay is decent, or probably more likely because he likes working creatively with flowers, all of which are motivators. However, the florist who recognizes that every customer will have a story; they buy flowers regularly as a sign of affection for someone they love; there's a special occasion being celebrated; there's a sad occasion being marked; there's someone in need of a bit of TLC, or whatever, will be inspired to provide an all-together different level of service. Simon Sinek's bestseller *Start with Why*, puts it simply: *"People don't buy WHAT you do, they buy WHY you do it."* As a leader, if you can talk with people to help them discover their *'why'*, you will increase their commitment exponentially. *Why* on earth would you not do that?

b. Extrinsic Motivation. **What** do you get out of doing this job? Essentially, this conversation is about the 'extrinsic motivators' in life such as money, promotion, perks, status, working conditions, security and personal development. They combine to play an important part in motivating people, so you ignore them at your peril. However, a few very notable limitations are worth pointing out:

- Research consistently evidences that the impact of extrinsic motivators tends to be short-lived. The boost of a pay rise fades quickly once your lifestyle has absorbed the extra income, and the new salary level no longer excites you. Man is indeed 'a wanting animal', and however much we have, we all soon want more. Don't make the mistake of trying to retain your best people with a 'pay to stay' strategy; eventually your funds will run out, and soon after so will your best people!

- Research evidence categorises many of these extrinsic rewards as 'hygiene factors', rather than 'motivators'. By this, they mean their impact on motivation relates more significantly to the de-motivation they cause when they are absent or inadequate, rather than the motivation they bring when they are present and correct. Few people will say: "I love working here because the office is so clean," yet many will become demotivated if the office is an unhealthy mess. Perhaps surprising, few people ever say: "I really enjoy my job because I'm paid well." Hardly anybody thinks that way for a sustained period, and yet most will become demotivated, even in a job they like, if they feel their pay isn't fair. So the message is, never under-estimate the importance of getting the 'hygiene factors' right, but don't think showering people with extrinsic rewards will make them more motivated. They may stick around to milk the rewards for as long as possible, but that is very different from being motivated.

The Secret of the Universe

If you had a way of massively increasing your colleague's motivation that didn't cost a penny and took virtually no time, would you use it? Well, you have, but you don't! Transactional Analysis introduced the concept of 'Strokes', defined as 'units of recognition'. Recognition, psychologists tell us, is the most basic human need, and this explains why *Strokes* are considered the 'Secret of the Universe'! In their total absence, it explains why solitary confinement is such an extreme punishment, or why when children bully others by isolating and ignoring them it has such a crushing effect, but flip the coin, and you have an incredibly positive tool at your disposal. Workplace surveys consistently rank 'Appreciation' as the #1 motivator; we all yearn to feel recognized and valued. We have discussed this over many years with hundreds of course delegates, and there is an interesting conundrum. Whilst most people comment that there have been many times when they haven't felt sufficiently appreciated, they almost all feel they themselves consistently show a high level of appreciation. That simply doesn't add up. The books don't balance, and the upshot is that most of us do not express our appreciation as fully or as frequently as we think.

In short, we have to raise our game. I know in response there will be those who say: "Sure, but it can all become a bit fake and insincere." My hope is that you will reflect for a moment before adopting that excuse because it is just an excuse. The truth is, most of us get nowhere near the point of looking fake, and even if we did, would it be so bad to be seen as generous with our praise? The impact of showing appreciation is immense, and all the evidence points to us doing so less often than we could and should. So, come on, let's all step it up!

Top Tip 1:

Make an informal reminder on a frequent basis to consider who deserves specific thanks for their effort and contribution. Be careful to avoid an artificial 'diary card' approach; people will sniff that a mile off. Equally, don't make it an exclusive club; your recognition has to be even-handed and fair. Commit to it because when someone has gone the extra mile, you must acknowledge it.

Top Tip 2:

Remember, the 'different strokes for different folks' mantra, so use your judgement to get it right. For some people a discrete and sincere 'thank you' is how they like to be appreciated, others love a public fanfare, and others will be fired up by a small token of appreciation. Use your judgement to get the 'stroke' right.

The Two Levers

18th century writer Samuel Johnson declared, *"There are two great movers of the human mind; the desire for good, and the fear of evil."*, and current phrases such as 'the carrot and stick' echo his view, as do concepts such as people being motivated both 'towards' a positive outcome and 'away from' a negative outcome. For example, when buying a car, to some extent you will be motivated 'towards' a vehicle that is shinier, higher-status, faster, more fuel-efficient, more reliable, safer or cheaper to maintain. To some extent you will be motivated away from your existing car which looks tired, compares badly with your neighbour's, lacks power, guzzles petrol, keeps breaking down, lacks basic safety features and is expensive to service.

The 'towards' and 'away from' levers relate to every aspect of life, and leaders need to judge the usefulness and appropriateness of each in their leadership efforts. For some colleagues, the positive influence of the 'carrot' will have far more effect, such as: "If you get involved in this project and perform well it will enable me to put you forward for promotion at your next review." For others, the threat of the 'stick' may work better, such as: "If you don't take up the opportunity to join this project your ability to contribute fully to the team will be eroded and that might force me to think about other resourcing options." Few would disagree that 'carrots' are more effective in most situations and more sustainable in all situations, than 'sticks'. However, it's naïve to think there aren't times when the stick has to be used; at times, it is only fair and honest to make people aware of the consequences of under-performance.

'Over-done Strengths'... A Golden Nugget

We finish this section on a cautionary note but one that offers us an incredible insight into how to encourage others to grow. Everybody should read this section!

As counter-intuitive as it may seem, it is essential not to *over-develop* a strength; beyond the point where ironically it becomes a weakness. By definition, *every* weakness can be attributed to an over-developed strength. For example, arrogant people are excessively confident; gullible people show too much trust and loyalty; abrasive people don't filter their comments and are hurtfully honest; smothering people are overly-nurturing ... and the list goes on.

This insight offers an extraordinary advantage when it comes to giving feedback and during development conversations. From this day forward you can delete any painful talk of 'weaknesses', which so often results in disappointment and defensiveness, and instead orient your development discussions more positively towards acknowledging a person's strength whilst also suggesting that they would benefit from 'dialing it down' a little. The conversation may go: "I really admire your drive and competitiveness, which the team benefits from on many occasions. However, there are times when I think you over-do it, and as a result alienate some of your colleagues. Let's talk about how you can dial this down a little so that it works well for everybody." That doesn't necessarily make it an easy conversation, but it's much better than: "I'm concerned about how self-oriented you are and how your competitiveness alienates the team." Simply, the brain finds it far easier to dial-down a strength, than it does to eliminate a weakness.

If you focus on weaknesses, you are always talking about a 'gap', something that is missing or wrong, and so needs to be corrected. On the contrary, recognising and approaching the issue as an 'over-developed strength' is more constructive and less critical, and makes it easier for people to acknowledge and respond to.

Section 3:
Key Leadership Skills

Chapters:

Just like the seasoned coach in our picture, the primary role of a coach is to help others see their potential, and for that reason the mirror is the key to the picture. Notice the coach is not 'telling' the athlete he could be better: he is enabling the athlete to 'see' it for himself.

There is a world of difference between these two approaches, and it makes coaching a contender for the 'most powerful leadership skill' award. For those leaders who aspire to be 'transformational' i.e. to really make a difference to people and their performance, coaching simply has to be a prominent part of their leadership style.

Coaching can seem counter-intuitive. Take our sports coach; if he 'knows' what will make that athlete better, many would argue it would be best simply to tell him. That surely would be most time efficient and effective. However, there are two flaws to this. First, the athlete then does not 'own' the advice and secondly, in all probability, the athlete will know full-well what he needs to do to become better! The coach's role, therefore, is to explore that second element. Only if he feels the athlete is missing some insights will he switch to the world of 'tell'.

The impact of coaching is immense, so let's explore it a bit more deeply.

26 centuries ago, Greek philosopher Anaximander made a remarkable proposal about the nature of our earth and its interaction with the celestial bodies that surrounded it. At that time, our understanding of our world consisted of only two dimensions. We stood on a flat earth and, in the (somewhat later) words of John Lennon, 'above us only sky'. Anaximander was unconvinced by this simplistic picture and was intrigued by the stars and planets in the night sky and the predictable movement of the sun. This led him to the extraordinary thought that the earth sat mysteriously suspended in mid-air, with these celestial bodies somehow revolving around our planet. Think how outrageous and illogical that thought must have seemed; we all know it is impossible to suspend anything in mid-air.

Regardless, subsequent philosophers extended Anaximander's theory, notably postulating that the shape of our earth was far more likely to be spherical than flat. However, the belief that the earth was positioned at the centre of the universe was never questioned, and that view was held for another two millennia. That was, until the 16th century mathematician and astronomer Nicolaus Copernicus proposed the unimaginable - that the sun, not the earth, lay at the heart of our universe. The concept of earth simply being one part of a 'solar system' drew contempt from the Christian churches. Lutheran reformer Philip Melanchthon berated Copernicus for his work, writing: "Wise rulers should have curbed such light-mindedness." Despite theologian resistance, Copernicus' proposal grew in evidence and his scientific findings rapidly became irrefutable.

In the centuries that followed, the resources and instrumentation available to study astronomy advanced beyond belief, and today we have evidence that the sun is in fact no more than a star. Astronomers estimate there are one hundred billion such stars in our galaxy, the majority of which are orbited by planets similar to our own. Further, through the latest and most advanced space exploration, it is now estimated that our galaxy may be just one of a billion, billion galaxies, sitting within the overall cosmos. Our planet is a speck of dust within our universe, and our universe is a speck of dust in the vastness of the cosmos. We have much to learn!

It is hard to comprehend the cosmos, so let's turn our attention closer to home, to our microscopic planet called 'earth'. By the middle of the second millennium AD, whilst it was viable for people to travel between countries, it was exceptionally rare to travel between continents. In fact, early maps from that age are notable for their blank spaces. Simply, the cartographers did not know what lay beyond their own territories. Ambitious and daring explorers such as Christopher Columbus, aided by emerging navigational and seafaring capabilities, set sail to address that. In 1492, Columbus set off westward from Spain into this empty void, expecting to reach Japan, the next landmass that the cartographers knew existed. Of course, he encountered instead an unknown continent, America!

Humankind's appetite to explore the earth continued to intensify over the centuries that followed. When the British Navy set off on expeditions, the military personnel were joined by inquisitive scientists, medics, geologists and a whole host of other academics, all intent on finding out more about our earth. In one such expedition, in 1831, HMS Beagle set sail for South America. On board was a young geology student named Charles Darwin. The rest, as they say, is history.

So what did Anaximander, Copernicus, Columbus and Darwin have in common? Simply, they were all prepared to challenge acknowledged truths, for the very reason that they accepted *they didn't have all the answers*. As a result, their inquisitive 'unknowing' minds never stopped exploring, and they never stopped learning.

The word *ignoramus* is an insulting term, used to infer a lack of knowledge or intellect. I recall during my strict schooling days that if I attempted to explain a wrong answer by saying "I thought ...," the sarcastic response would be: *"You know what 'Thought' did? He followed a muck cart and thought he was going to a wedding."* It's an odd expression, and a long-winded way of saying: "You're stupid!" It is also a profoundly poor way to teach. In similar vein, I hear on occasion my least-favourite expression: *"I don't suffer fools gladly."* Usually proclaimed in self-righteous tones, it invariably reveals more about the speaker than those it is aimed at. However, there might just be a silver lining here; *ignoramus* stems from Latin, meaning "we do not know". First used in the French legal profession almost 500 years ago, when a jury might conclude: 'We do not know' (in most cases due to insufficient evidence). Think about this for a moment. It is that very 'not knowing' that has always compelled the greatest thinkers to explore and discover. Indeed, the likes of Anaximander all spoke of theories which they *thought* might be correct, rather than of certainties. They were never deluded by any notion of omniscience. In fact, it was their *not knowing* that enabled them to know so much.

"Oh, what idiots we all have been. This is just as it must be."
Niels Bohr

This type of 'enquiring' mindset is critical for today's leaders. The 'lifelong learning' graph shown in Chapter 7 illustrated how profoundly learning has changed over recent decades, and how learning is about a constant quest to keep at the 'leading edge'. In our coaching work, we often discuss with people how they balance their approach between giving and seeking information, as reflected by the spectrum shown below:

Knowing   Enquiring

We believe this conversation is one of the most important for leaders today. At one end of the spectrum are those who are certain they know the answer, and that their view counts for more than anyone else's. There may well be times when there is some truth to that, but it is a dangerous 'default setting', and the pitfalls are expressed brilliantly in Robert Graves' poem 'In Broken Images':

He is quick, thinking in clear images;
I am slow, thinking in broken images

He becomes dull, trusting his clear images;
I become sharp, mistrusting my broken images.

Trusting his images, he assumes their relevance;
Mistrusting my images, I question their relevance.

Assuming their relevance, he assumes the fact;
Questioning their relevance, I question the fact.

When the fact fails him, he questions his senses;
When the fact fails me, I approve my senses.

He continues quick and dull in his clear images;
I continue slow and sharp in my broken images.

He in a new confusion of his understanding;
I in a new understanding of my confusion.

Referring back to the four leadership themes in the book's Introduction, we can easy see that 'Knowing' leaders are found most commonly within the *Domination* and *Negotiation* workplaces. On the contrary, the 'Enquiring' leaders tend towards the *Inspiration* and, most commonly, the *Co-Creation* workplaces. 'Enquiring leaders' are energised by the prospect of exploring solutions with colleagues, and not at all perturbed by their own 'ignorance'. Instead, they hold firm to the belief that the answer will be found collectively. People are inspired by these self-confident leaders who show genuine respect by consulting their colleagues. In response, people willingly offer all their talents and ideas.

What is coaching?

John Whitmore defined coaching as: *"Unlocking a person's potential to maximize their performance. It is helping them to learn rather than teaching them."* This is echoed by author Bob Nelson's view that *"You get the best results from others, not by lighting the fire underneath them, but by building the fire within them."* And so, coaching is about exploring with a person what it is they would like to develop, and providing encouragement for them to embrace whatever learning they believe is necessary to achieve that. Please re-read that last sentence; what do you notice? I hope what leaps out is that it's all about *them*, not about *you*. It is not about your goals, and it is not about your advice. It is about the coachee, and it should feel like an engaging conversation: not a performance review.

"I learned not from those who taught me, but from those who talked with me." Saint Augustine

Coaching can be defined as a development conversation that is underpinned by optimism and encouragement, fuelled by a genuine belief in a person's potential. It is heavily focused on the person you are coaching, and thus the airspace is owned predominantly by them. The coach's sole intent is to help the coachee explore how they can achieve their goals. The two main tools of the coaching profession are 'great questions' and 'active listening'. For too long we have viewed speaking as an active process, and listening as a passive process, yet the opposite is true. We can all happily talk for hours, simply regurgitating what we already know, and at the worst we may get a sore throat. On the contrary, try listening for hours and notice how exhausting it is; listening is hard work, and beyond a point will give you a sore head. The best coaches have learned to listen, deeply, not just to people's words, but also to how they say them, what they emphasise, what they omit, and what visual clues arise too. For the minority who develop the orientation and skill to do those things, the impact is profound. If I could give just one tip to leaders it would be: "Never miss a good opportunity to shut up!" We encourage aspiring coaches to follow the acronym ZULU more often i.e. *'Zip Up & Listen Up'*!

It is surely no coincidence that 'silent' is an anagram of 'listen', and it is a great reminder to those who wish to coach that silence truly is 'golden'. Those who listen to you are showing you huge respect.

There are numerous coaching frameworks in use today. However, most are closely related to the most commonly used framework - 'GROW'. The GROW acronym, developed by coaches Graham Alexander, Alan Fine, and Sir John Whitmore provides a simple approach to a coaching conversation. The sequential steps are:

• clarify the person's **G**oal
• establish their current **R**eality
• explore what **O**ptions may help them close that gap
• ensure that they have the **W**ill to take those actions

GROW should serve as a route map, not be a straight-jacket. Its prime purpose is to help the coaching conversation stay on track and reach a purposeful outcome.

Don't confuse Coaching with Mentoring

Homer's epic poem Odyssey tells the mythical story of Odysseus' journey from the state of Ithaca, where he was king, to join his fellow Greeks in fighting the Trojan War. Odysseus at that time had a young son, Telemachus, and so he made plans for him to be guided and nurtured through his formative years by his wise old friend, Mentor. Odysseus' absence would, it turned out, last twenty years, due to the length of the War and the intervention of an angered sea-god Neptune. Upon his return, Odysseus reunited with Telemachus, and together they repelled those who had sought to take the King's crown in Odysseus' absence.

This story from Greek mythology (a modern interpretation, and rather more positive than Homer's original text) provides the root to the word *Mentor*, which refers to someone who has greater knowledge and experience than another, and who uses that to provide wise guidance and counsel. In other words, it involves the giving of advice, often very general advice, by someone who has both the experience and wisdom to dispense it. A mentor does not have to be older than the other person (the mentee), although in practice that most often is the case. Mentoring is a powerful and positive aspect of support, and the best performers I have known share the same enthusiasm to seek and secure helpful mentoring.

Whilst in everyday life the terms 'coaching' and 'mentoring' are often used interchangeably, let's be clear, they shouldn't; the two approaches to providing support are entirely distinct. A mentor is a trusted adviser, and so provides insights and knowledge: a coach helps to explore what already lies with you. I'm not saying that coaches *never* give advice: sometimes they do. However, it should be reserved for those very occasional situations where genuinely that is needed in order to help the coachee progress their thinking. As such, advice-giving is the last resort for a coach, who will always encourage others to find their own solution. The irrefutable logic supporting the power of coaching is all about 'ownership'; when a course of action is *your* solution, you *own* the solution, and as a result will be innately more committed to it.

In practical terms, you will most commonly see the inter-weaving of coaching and mentoring in sports settings, where sports coaches – and they invariably are called 'coaches', not 'mentors' - will both try to bring out the best in others, whilst also offer specific advice on techniques, nutrition, psychology etc. Both types of intervention are helpful, but you should at least be aware whether you are coaching or mentoring, and do not confuse the two. If you do not have that awareness the danger is our natural propensity to dispense advice surfaces far too frequently, and any hope of harnessing the incredible power of coaching is lost.

Action Point:

When you are having a coaching conversation with someone and you find yourself drawn to give advice, or to give the 'answer', don't! Instead, pause and wait, and continue to enquire what the other person thinks themselves. You will be amazed how often the solution - or at least the vast majority of it - sits within them.

Mind your language

You can always spot an experienced coach by the language they use. It is invariably less directive and more enquiring than typical 'management speak'. Coaching is also non-judgemental, although that is not about dodging the issue or avoiding confrontation: when it is necessary to be direct a coach will be direct. Rather, it is about showing respect and trust, avoiding a 'Parent:Child' exchange, and ensuring those being coached retain ownership of the issue and the resolution. This shift towards a coaching-style language is typified by the examples below:

Instruct	Involve
I want you to ...	How do you feel about ...
Why are you struggling?	What are the blockers?
You're wrong about that	I have a different view
That's not possible	How can you overcome ...
You made a mistake	How can we fix this?
Listen to me	Let's discuss this
You're not being realistic	I have some practical concerns
I've already told you ...	I still think ...
This is how you do it	How do you plan to do it?
I'll talk you through step-by-step	Can I offer some advice?
We need this by Monday	Can you deliver by Monday?
That's not going to happen	I would be concerned about ...

Please don't make the mistake of thinking this is just semantics. Choose your words carefully; they make a difference. Needless to say, your words have to be authentic; this is not a game of fakery. The result, you will find, is that using coaching language will open a more constructive and enabling conversation. Relationships will be closer, trust will be higher, and people's development and performance will accelerate.

Coaching makes learning stick

Forward-thinking organisations make a priority of training and developing their staff. Organisations across the globe currently spend an estimated £300 billion each year on training, which includes an average developed-world organisation spending around £1,000 per employee. It is a huge investment, and one that is essential for the success of the business and for job satisfaction. Ensuring the spend delivers a good return on investment is vital, and by 'good return', that means the new learning is retained and applied effectively.

Unfortunately, evidence reveals that way too little of our training sticks. Research dating as far back at 1980 shows that following a presentation of a theory or description of a skill, only about 10% of people went on to apply that learning. Even when people were given a demonstration of the skill, allowed to practise it, and receive feedback on their performance, that figure only increased to around 20%. We should not be hugely surprised by that. I use the example of comedy nights that I love going to, and how I always try to remember as many of the jokes as possible. I am always astounded at how few I can remember the next day. Even when I've really enjoyed the show, the jokes just don't stick.

The good news, though, is that various research initiatives have since established a way to substantially boost that application of learning, and the secret lies in 'on-the-job' coaching. Amazingly, in cases where training delegates return to the workplace and are actively coached by colleagues who take a keen interest in their learning, the application of learning *quadruples*. That is an incredible statistic, but it does make sense. Having people around you who ask: "How did the course go?"; "What did you find most interesting, and useful?"; "How will you apply that?"; "Were there any bits you found difficult, that I could help you with?" etc. all will quite clearly have a profound effect on the application of the learning. The tangible impact of coaching could not be more transparent.

A 'shout out' for Optimism

Nelson Mandela famously survived 27-years incarcerated in a prison cell and then went on to teach others how to lay down the gun. The following is an excerpt from his inaugural speech as President of South Africa, in 1994 (which he adapted from American writer Marianne Williamson):

Our deepest fear is not that we are inadequate. Our deepest fear is that we are powerful beyond measure. It is our light, not our darkness, that most frightens us. We ask ourselves, who am I to be brilliant, gorgeous, talented and fabulous? Actually, who are you NOT to be? You are a child of God. Your playing small doesn't serve the world. There's nothing enlightened about shrinking so that other people won't feel insecure around you. We were born to manifest the glory of God. That is within us. It's not just in some of us; it's in EVERYONE!

Consider for a moment what it means to reach our potential. By 'potential', I mean being the best you could possibly be at a chosen pursuit, whether that is sales, presenting, leadership, speaking a foreign language, golf, chess, parenting etc. Then consider the question: "At what percentage of their potential do most people operate." Admittedly, that's so broad and subjective a question it is impossible to put a specific number on it. Over the years, however, we have asked hundreds of delegates that very question, and answers almost invariably range between 20-60%, averaging at around 40%. Who knows what the correct answer is, but the relatively consistent estimates point to one belief; just about everyone has the capacity for *huge* performance improvement.

"The greater danger for most of us is not that our aim is too high and we miss it, but that it is too low and we reach it." Michelangelo

Whilst these low estimates might be interpreted as negative, or even critical, actually they expose amazing optimism. This optimism is the foundation stone for all coaching; without it, coaching would be pointless. If I believe you have so much more within you, I am even more compelled to offer you the support you need to release that potential. Conversely, if you didn't believe in a person's potential, then why on earth would you invest your time and energy in coaching them? Please don't think coaching will work every time; there will be occasions when our coaching may not achieve as much as we might hope, but we must try for others. As Charles Handy writes in his book *The Hungry Spirit*: "Optimists are always prey to disappointment, but life without hope is dismal." As a coach, you have to have both the optimism and the resilience to retain your inherent belief in people's potential.

As the diagram below shows, optimists and pessimists don't lead separate lives because, we all experience both outlooks at different times, and also everybody's mindset merges somewhat into the 'Not Sure' mid-zone. The challenge for all of us is to make a shift to the left, towards optimism. What have you got to lose?

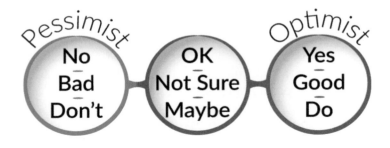

You may tell me that you know what your potential is. However, with genuine respect, I honestly doubt you do. It was French philosopher René Descartes who famously wrote: *"Cogito ergo sum,"* meaning 'I think, therefore I am'. His main point was to challenge whether any of us actually 'know' anything, his hypothesis being that all that we 'knew' was, in fact, what we all 'think'. Let's sidestep his philosophical point and consider the practical implication of this. If I think I am a kind person, then in my mind that is 'true' also, at least as far as I am concerned. If I think I have achieved well in life, that becomes 'true' too! In reality, of course, all of those things are *not* necessarily true; they are merely what I think. Despite that, what we think drives everything we do, and will influence how our lives play out. If I think I have more potential, then that is 'true', and I will raise my game to release that potential. If I think I have peaked, then I will shift to cruise control, and my performance will plateau.

Your first and most critical role as a coach is to help people see the extent of their potential. As Susan Howson put it: *"I AM - the two most powerful words in the world, for whatever we put after them becomes our reality."* Helping people put aside their limiting beliefs, and see the reality of their potential, is the greatest gift a coach can give. It sets people on an empowered learning journey, where they confidently drive their own development. They may need external support along the way but, in the main, their improvements come from within. As Chris Argyris put it: *"No one can develop anyone else apart from himself. The door to development is locked from inside."*

⚛ Coaching Insights:

As you turn the dial up in your efforts to make coaching a bigger part of your leadership repertoire, I offer below some golden tips to becoming more effective:

Resolve to be a sounding board. When you enter a meeting, focus primarily on asking open questions and provoking deeper thinking on the conversation topic. Resist the temptation to keep providing solutions.

Create the right environment. Generally, this should be a neutral space away from distractions where you can be 100% 'present'. The style should be relaxed, informal and positive. Above all, the conversation has to be 'Adult:Adult' in tone. Those who exert their authority lose the 'commitment of coaching' and find it replaced by its poor substitute, the 'compliance of control'.

Ditch the direction. Admittedly, it *is* necessary and a key part of a leader's role to at times to set direction, but not when coaching. This is because directing promotes dependency. Instead, resolve to give less advice and fewer answers. Help others see that they are empowered and trusted, and encourage them to share their ideas.

Build high-trust relationships. Successful coaching requires the openness and honesty that comes from having a strong sense of 'connection', allowing people to be upfront about their development needs. That professional friendship enables honest and challenging conversations, and encourages the sharing of helpful feedback.

Lose your ego. In cases where you are also the manager of your coachee, it's only when you have the inner confidence to put your status aside that you can dispense with the need to take control of the outcome. Remember it is about *them*; it is *their* outcome, and *they* should control it.

Be action-oriented. Whilst you want the conversation to be relaxed and informal, you also need to influence others to step forward and 'step up'. So make sure you focus your line of enquiry on questions such as: "What can you do to progress this?" and "When might you get that done?" As Mark Twain put it: "*The secret of getting ahead is getting started.*" There is a golden question that coaches lean on heavily when actions have been identified and agreed, and that is: "On a scale of 1-10, how committed are you to do x, y & z?" It places a strong focus on the 'doing', and my advice is to be wary of any response that is 8 or less! Less than 8, and you have to question is this really a goal they want to achieve, or did they really identify the 'right' actions to achieve that goal.

Feedback Effectively. You might have heard the quote about feedback being 'the breakfast of champions'. It sounds cliché, but it is absolutely true! The hardest person to judge is yourself, so everyone needs to hear the perspective of others. If you really want to help someone grow, have the courage to share your insights. More of that in the next chapter.

It starts NOW. It is often said that the process of personal change takes years. Well, forget that, and coach people to be the person they want to be, NOW! I don't mean you can be CEO now, or run a marathon now, but you *can* live the life that will get you there, starting right NOW! Follow the advice of inventor Charles Kettering who said: *"Believe and act as if it were impossible to fail."* (Caution: Skydivers, please ignore that last bit!)

Cautionary Note: If the biggest mistake a leader can make is to *never* coach, then the second biggest mistake is to *always* coach! There are few management styles worse than the '24/7 Coach'. Coaching works well in scenarios where people need to believe in themselves more and, in truth, *do* have most of the answers within them. Most people who aspire, let's say, to get fit, know 99% of the ways to do just that. The role of the coach is not to set their diet and exercise regime; they already know the gym is better than the sofa and that a piece of fruit is better than a bag of crisps. The coach's role instead is to help them visualize and articulate more clearly for themselves what they mean by 'get fitter'. Then it is to help them talk through which of the many ways to get fit appeal to them most and, therefore, which they will commit to.

However, in some scenarios, the other person may *not* have all the answers and may not be entirely sure where to get them. In that case, it would be far more helpful to give them direct advice and guidance, by telling them *what* they need to do and *how* they should do it. You wouldn't coach a drowning man to swim; you dive in and rescue him! Trying to coach a person who does not have the abilities or insights to achieve their goals will achieve nothing but frustration.

I remember thinking, if one more person tells me: *"Feedback is a gift,"* I may not be responsible for my actions! I'm glad it never came to that because I have come right around the circle and am now the biggest advocate of that saying - OK, admitting that it *is* a tad cheesy!

Think about the flipside for a moment. If you really want to hold someone back, limit their prospects, and ensure they never reach their potential, then it is a great idea to step away from them and deny them any feedback.

Think of any pursuit, in or out of work, when you have had someone who helped you develop. Those people gave their time to guide you; to tell you when you were doing 'too much of this' or 'too little of that'; what new things you should try and what habits you should shake-off. You needed that feedback.

Somehow, in the workplace, that sort of free-flowing and natural feedback slows dramatically, or even stops. It's illogical; if people don't know how they're doing or how they can improve, how can they possibly develop themselves?

Of course, our reasons for avoiding feedback conversations rarely include the desire to constrain someone. More frequently, it is about not having the courage to enter a difficult conversation, unsure how it will be received and the impact it will have on the relationship. It is entirely understandable to be concerned about those things because attempts to give feedback, at times, do back-fire. Regardless, if you accept that a big part of the role of leadership is to help others grow, then you have to step up and show that courage.

An exercise we run on our training courses is often described by participants as one of those 'lightbulb moments' in life. We take four volunteers out of the room and tell them they will be asked to come in one at a time, blindfolded, and undertake a simple specified task, such as to throw a pen in a box. We simultaneously brief the remainder of the group who remain in the training room that they must act in four different prescribed ways in the case of each volunteer. When the first volunteer enters the room, the group's brief is to be totally silent. Unsurprisingly, the volunteer cannot complete the task; they have no idea where the box is! The second volunteer enters the room, and this time the group's brief is to be critical, shouting comments like: "Hurry up", "It's an easy task, just get on with it" and "Even a kid could do that." Again, needless to say, they can't complete the task. The third volunteer enters the room, and this time the group have been briefed to be really positive, but only with bland general comments such as "you're great", "we believe in you", and "we know you can do it." Again, despite all that encouragement, they simply cannot do the task. Finally, the fourth volunteer is ushered in, and this time the group have been briefed to provide whatever input and feedback that would help. Without exception, the groups all then provide precise guidance, allowing the volunteer swiftly to complete the task.

It's an exaggerated activity of course, and may seem perfectly obvious, but I promise you that seeing it in action does expose the learning point that a person's performance can never improve without appropriate feedback. As every volunteer from the first three scenarios tells us, their experience was really frustrating. The experience of the fourth volunteer is, of course, the opposite; they succeed and invariably are grateful for the helpful feedback.

Now, I ask you to reflect for a moment how many times you have observed colleagues perform below par, yet you ducked the issue and just didn't tell them. Imagine the scenario where a colleague struggles when making presentations because he's too monotone, gets breathless, doesn't use eye contact, jingles coins in his pocket, uses too many visuals, overruns his time slot, doesn't allow for questions, is badly prepared etc. Instead of taking him to one side afterwards and saying: "Hey, can I please give you some advice" you walk away, part of the collective who will forever view him as 'the guy who does bad presentations', and deny him the insights that would help him improve. You took the easy option, and you failed in your leadership.

🏵 Action Point:

Resolve to make giving feedback a routine part of your leadership approach, and ensure that your intent always is constructive. There will be occasions when it may not be welcomed but, most of the time, for the majority of people, it will be a positive and beneficial experience which they will appreciate.

There are many established frameworks for giving feedback well, and we use the simple and effective AID model most frequently, as shown in the diagram overleaf, together with an example of how this might be used in practice:

Action
Tell them what they did, in specific terms.

Impact
Tell them what the impact of that was.

Do
Give constructive advice about what they should do in future.

Action: *"Your voice sounded flat when you spoke to the customer, and you didn't respond to her comment about the problem she had had last time"* is much more helpful than: *"Your customer service isn't very good."*

Impact: *"I think she concluded we're not interested in her custom and might decide to take her business elsewhere."*

Do: *"Ask more questions to demonstrate your interest, and use a more varied tone of voice, which will demonstrate you are fully engaged. Listen carefully to their answers and if customers raise specific concerns make a point of exploring and resolving them."*

The rest of this section looks at more general themes for getting it right.

Don't present 'Rights' and 'Wrongs'

*An elderly rabbi was approached by two men having a heated argument. The rabbi calmly asked the first man for his opinion on the issue and, having listened, declared: "You are right!" He then did the same for the second man and again, having listened, he exclaimed: "You also are right!" The rabbi's wife, who had been listening from outside the door, suddenly protested: "They cannot **both** be right!", to which the rabbi responded: "And you are right too!"*

The story of the rabbi teaches us to be cautious of 'absolute truths', because these rarely exist. 13th-century Persian poet, Rumi, declared: *"Out beyond right and wrong there is a place. I will meet you there."* The Greeks held the same view, referring to the mid-point between two extremes, or points of view, as the 'Golden Mean'. Socrates referred to it in relation to education, suggesting that too much emphasis on gymnastics creates a hard and aggressive person, whilst too much emphasis on music creates a soft person. Yet, engaging in both pursuits produced a broader and more-balanced individual, which we might summarise as 'all virtues lie midpoint on a continuum'.

In life, we very rarely deal in absolute rights or absolute wrongs. Instead, we should recognise that people and situations are unique, and be more flexible in our views. The best 'middle ground' may not always be precisely mid-way, but it will lie somewhere between the two starting positions.

Just as no two people are the same, similarly, no two approaches will be identical. As the old saying goes: "It's better to be a first class version of yourself than a second class version of someone else."

So, as a feedback giver, don't fall into the trap of thinking others must do precisely as you do. It always serves the feedback receiver best when you offer ideas about a *direction* in which they should move, rather than a rigid "you must do it precisely like this." To a colleague who presents nervously, it is invariably more enabling to advise them to: "Try to slow your pace of talking," than: 'You need to speak at 110 words per minute.' That statistic may have some validity, but everyone is different. Guide them in the right direction, rather than bind them to a formula you happen to believe in.

In conclusion, unless you are dealing with precise factual issues, show balance and open-mindedness. Prescribe less: guide more.

The 5:1 Rule

However positive your intent, and however well you refine your feedback technique, the underlying message of developmental feedback is: "You need to up your game!" We all have thinner skin than we care to admit, and so giving such feedback always runs the risk of causing people to feel that we are picking on their faults. Indeed, we will all have encountered examples where that is true, when a feedback giver's focus has become overly-weighted towards negative aspects. When that happens, as Tim Rath explains in his book *StrengthsFinder 2.0*, we are "taking the line of *most* resistance" when people become inclined to reject our suggestions. This is not to say we should ignore factors that genuinely hold people back or 'derail' them, because feedback relating to those factors can be transformational. However, it does imply there is some vital groundwork to be done upfront if we want our well-intended developmental feedback to be taken constructively.

Research indicates that most people need to receive positive and developmental feedback in an approximate ratio of 5:1 respectively, if they are to trust the giver's intent and be genuinely open to the feedback. A good dose of common sense is needed when interpreting this ratio; clearly it is not implying we can deliver five trivial bits of positive feedback, and then slam that person with a huge criticism. Rather, it is prompting us to make a habit of expressing genuine appreciation on a regular basis, so that we build a foundation of trust and respect.

"Everyone wants to be appreciated, so if you appreciate someone, don't keep it a secret." Mary Kay Ash

The business tycoon Sir David Tang was widely admired for his warmth and refined etiquette, and his advice included that you should never write the words 'thank you' in a Thank You card. His reasoning was that the words are too bland, almost meaningless. Instead, the writer should be specific about why they wish to extend their thanks, and in doing so their message becomes far more personal and impactful. In precisely the same way, feedback becomes so much more valuable and impactful when it is specific. Providing the feedback: "I think you demonstrated such a pride in our company when you spoke to that customer" is so much more helpful than: "I think you handled that call really well." Positive feedback strengthens relationships, but being specific in your praise has the added advantage of reinforcing the behaviours you would like to encourage.

Dinah Craik's adapted Arabian proverb below, expresses wonderfully how the inter-personal trust and respect that develops through such positive and reinforcing behaviours allows relationships to be open and honest, with minimal risk that unguarded comments will cause damage:

> *Oh the joy ... the inexpressible comfort*
> *Of feeling safe with a person*
> *Having neither to measure words, nor weigh thoughts*
> *Pouring them all out just as they are,*
> *Chaff & grain together*
> *Certain that a loving hand will sift through,*
> *Keep what is worth keeping,*
> *And with a breath of kindness ... blow the rest away.*

The 5:1 ratio lays that positive foundation, and both *you* and *they* will find the sharing of developmental feedback a far more positive and effective experience. When you reach that stage, feedback truly *is* 'a gift'!

Criticism isn't Feedback

I read an interesting moral tale a number of years back about a young boy who would at times lash out at others with unkind words. The boy's mother, struggling to teach her son the error of his ways, sought the help of her parents. The boy's grandfather came up with an idea to help his grandson learn the impact of his outbursts. Every time the boy had been unkind he would have to hammer a huge nail into a wooden block. The boy assumed this was his grandfather's way of encouraging him to let off steam, and he quite enjoyed it. But after numerous tiring hammering episodes he began to lose interest in this task and so began to be more considerate towards his friends. Indeed, he even developed the goodwill to apologise when any occasional unkindness did surface.

That was when his grandmother stepped in. She asked him to fetch the block filled with nails and told him he must now pull them all out. This was a much harder task than pounding them in, but after a huge struggle he eventually levered them all out. His grandmother hugged him and said: "I appreciate your efforts, but I want you to know an apology is like pulling out one of these nails. Look at the wood; the holes are still there, and the board will never be the same. Please don't be someone who puts holes in others."

It is a great story, not just for kids(!), to illustrate how criticism impacts so negatively and enduringly on people. Far from being a candid, but well-intended, message that helps people to improve, criticism lingers and festers, with little or no positive outcome. All too often, in the busy-ness of life, we can take short cuts when giving feedback. Maybe we don't lay the positive groundwork or maybe we don't use an effective process such as AID. The result is we demoralise and alienate people, rather than help them. Whilst it can be very helpful to constructively critique a person, please use your good judgement to avoid the sort of criticism that damages confidence, breaks relationships and stifles people's growth. If you are a naturally critical person, keep in mind author Leo Aikman's words: *"You can tell more about a person by what he says about others, than you can by what others say about him."*

"Self-esteem is so delicate a flower that praise tends to make it bloom, while discouragement often nips it in the bud." Alex F. Osborn

Feeding Forward

The phrase *Feedforward* has attracted much attention over recent years, and refers to the process of looking ahead and providing someone with ideas and suggestions for how they can develop their capabilities for future opportunities and challenges. Being forward-looking, constructive and relevant, feedforward unsurprisingly has become acknowledged as a high-impact leadership technique. Who wouldn't appreciate those insights and ideas? In effect, you are doing just the 'D' of the AID model i.e. "This is what I think you should do." Feedforward also has an element of 'self-fulfilling prophesy' about it; if you think you will fail a job interview, you will lower your expectations and preparations, and thus be more likely to fail. Thankfully, the reverse is true also. If I advise you on the best way to approach a forthcoming Sales meeting, then by adapting accordingly and applying that approach you will raise your expectations and competence, and you will be more likely to succeed. In summary, good *feedforward* creates a 'virtuous circle'.

But a word of caution: *Feedforward* lacks any reference to the past, a past that provides reference points for how people's strategies have worked out to date and may well offer evidence to suggest why an adapted or alternative strategy might be useful. Without these supporting insights, feedforward suggestions may carry less weight. And the integrity that lies behind an honest exchange of views is unquestionably part of the journey towards a high-trust relationship.

Rather than debate whether feedback or feedforward is better, let's agree they both have a worthy place in a leader's toolkit.

Feedback is a Two-way Street

Given you appreciate the immense value of feedback, you would be mad not to seek it for yourself! Aside from the insights you will gain, your role-modelling will influence those around you also to be open to feedback. It is a clear case of 'behaviour breeding behaviour'.

I would like to share just a few examples of feedback I have received and how useful they have been to me. Many years ago, a team member with whom I had a great relationship told me: "You sound so miserable when I phone you that I hesitate before calling you, and I think others do too." Ouch, that hurt! I'm relieved to say, part of her point was: "and that's in total contrast to how you are face-to-face." It might sound a trivial piece of feedback, but it was having an impact, and yet I was completely unaware. I could recognise her point was valid, and I reflected about how I do indeed have a low preference for telephone conversations. It was enough for me to make sure I 'upped my game' and stopped giving off such a poor first impression. We remain good friends, and I will always be grateful she stepped up and told me.

On another occasion, my boss at the time challenged me with the question: "Whose standards do you work to?" In brief, his observation was I seemed to be exceptionally drawn to deliver objectives and standards that were set for me, but I didn't seem to set any of my own. It was a deep insight that I mused over for some time, eventually coming to the conclusion that his observations were actually quite far from the truth. However, I did take something powerful from the message, that I needed to be more explicit about *my* personal objectives and standards. After all, if he couldn't see them how could he know I had them?

⊛ Action Point:

As a leader, be an enthusiastic seeker of feedback, and never offer excuses in response – that is the best way to ensure you don't receive any more! Instead, reflect upon the feedback and be grateful that a colleague has had the honesty and courage to offer it. Offer colleagues a coffee in return for their insights into how you perform. I find it helpful to put a framework around it, such as: "What are the three things about me you think I should improve or change?" To honourably seek feedback reaps so many rewards, and if you are brave enough as a leader, here is my favourite feedback question: "What's it like being on the receiving end of me?" Trust me, you'll be surprised at some of the answers you get back, but the insights they provide will be invaluable in targeting your development efforts. Go on, be bold!

Don't push for Perfection

A water bearer in India had two large pots, each hung on an end of a pole which he carried across his shoulders. One of the pots had a crack in it, and while the other pot was perfect and always delivered a full portion of water at the end of the long walk from the stream to the master's house, the cracked pot always arrived only half full. For two years this went on daily, with the bearer each time delivering only one and a half pots of water in his master's house.

The cracked pot spoke to the water bearer one day by the stream: "I am ashamed of myself, and I want to apologise to you." "Why?" asked the bearer, "what are you ashamed of?" "For these past two years, I have been able to deliver only half my load because this crack in my side causes water to leak out all the way back to your master's house. Because of my flaws, you get only half of the benefit." The water bearer felt sorry for the old cracked pot, and replied: "As we return to the master's house, I want you to notice the beautiful flowers along the path."

As they went up the hill, the old cracked pot took notice of the sun warming the beautiful wild flowers on the side of the path, and this cheered it some. But at the end of the trail, it still felt bad because it had again leaked out half its load. The bearer said to the pot: "Did you notice that there were flowers only on your side of the path? That's because I have always known about your flaw, and I took advantage of it. I planted flower seeds on your side of the path, and every day while we walk back from the stream, you've watered them. For two years I have been able to pick these beautiful flowers to decorate my master's table. Without you being just the way you are, he would not have had this beauty to grace his house."

It sounds odd to admire imperfections, however we should all be wary of the trap of perfection. High standards are an essential component of leadership; after all, who would admire a leader who settled for mediocrity? Perfection, though, is a different matter because it leads us down a long and frustrating path to inevitable failure. There has to be a limit to our endeavours in any one area, because time and energy are finite resources.

"Perfection is not attainable, but if we chase perfection we can catch excellence." Vince Lombardi

Perfectionism can serve us badly in several ways:

- The 'Law of Diminishing Returns' constantly erodes the productivity of perfectionists. The countless hours polishing every piece of work so often could be more productively applied elsewhere.

- Those who pursue perfectionism too far, fall into the 'over-developed strengths' camp. The strength of having an eye-for-detail turns into the weakness of being pedantic and obsessive.

- Perfectionism can result in excessive self-orientation i.e. *my* work has to be perfect, so I will spend 100% of my time on it. As a consequence, you fail to support your colleagues.

- Perfectionists hold such high standards that they insist on unhelpful comparisons with those who happen to truly excel at that aspect of performance. By all means, be inspired by such people, but don't become obsessed with always matching them. Play to *your* strengths, not theirs.

Also, remember that imperfections can themselves be a positive. They make us more human, and our vulnerability makes us more approachable. Allowing colleagues to support us in areas where we are less competent can be a really rewarding experience that contributes to healthy relationships and teamworking. In being less-than-perfect, we almost invariably find there are compensating factors elsewhere. For example, the person who can be frustratingly unplanned, might also be the person who copes best with unforeseen events. After all, their preferred way of working means they become adept at the spontaneity and urgency needed to handle those situations!

Perfection is an illusion, and relentlessly pursuing it leads to frustration, exhaustion and misery. If you choose to pursue an exceptionally narrow focus, such as elite sports or a specific field of science, then I accept you will need an intense dedication towards exceptional standards. But most of us are required to bring a vast range of capabilities to our lives and, in that context, perfectionism serves us badly.

"Ouch!" When it came to conflict handling strategies, 'Iron' Mike Tyson didn't have the most-subtle approach. Forget the craft and trickery of Ali, the lightning speed and defence of Mayweather, or the relentless jab and ring craft of Klitschko. 'Iron Mike' had just one strategy; he was going to walk straight through you! It was an effective strategy for someone with such explosive power, but it is only one strategy, and it won't work every time.

As a Vietnamese proverb puts it: *"Those who fight fire with fire, burn their houses down twice as fast."* When it comes to conflict we have to be much more flexible in our approach and develop a range of strategies that help us resolve the issue.

There is always a way

A Middle Eastern fable tells of the dilemma of a father who decides to leave his 17 camels to his three sons. To the eldest son he left half, to the middle son he left a third, and to the youngest son he left a ninth. The sons immediately entered a difficult negotiation, because 17 doesn't divide by 2, 3 or 9. The sons' dilemma raged and tempers rose. In desperation, they approached a wise old lady with their dilemma. She thought about their problem for a long time and finally came back to the sons and said: "I don't know if I can help, but if you want, you can have my camel." And, with that, she gave it to them, so they now had 18. So the eldest son took half i.e. 9 camels. The middle son took a third i.e. 6 camels. And the youngest son took a ninth i.e. 2 camels. The sons now had 9+6+2 camels, totalling 17 camels; and were all happy. And the remaining camel? They gave it back to the wise old woman!

Sometimes making progress is about aligning people, and helping them overcome what seems like opposing agendas. I first encountered the camel fable in Roger Fisher and William Ury's best-selling book on negotiating *Getting to Yes*. Whilst the story is founded on the incorrect mathematical assumption that a half, plus a third, plus a ninth, equals one (they don't, they equal seventeen eighteenths), it is a great example of how those skilled in conflict resolution can intervene in seemingly hopeless negotiations to help people find a way forward. As Fisher and Ury go on to explain, conflict occurs when two or more people hold a clear and opposing view. However, there is always a *third view*; either middle ground or a different way of approaching the issue. It is the people who have the skill and will to explore those options who are best at handling conflict.

Conflict has a purpose ... Embrace it!

"I've learned that pleasing everyone is impossible, but pissing everyone off, that's a piece of cake." Anon

It is no surprise that we are conditioned to see conflict as negative and to be avoided if at all possible. When it does arise, we naturally view the other person as being plain difficult. Often it feels either awkward or stressful - a situation that we would really rather not be in. However, we should think twice before ducking our heads. As Charles Spurgeon put it: *"Our anxiety does not empty tomorrow of its sorrow, but only empties today of its strength."* Confronting conflict is rarely easy, yet we should recognise that conflict fundamentally is about two people having a different opinion. There are good reasons to see that as both constructive and beneficial. Think about all those stimulating social occasions when you debate with friends which is the best sports team; which political party deserves your vote; which diet will provide the most health benefits etc. Not only are those conversations stimulating and enjoyable, they are wonderful learning opportunities too, but only if people are prepared to listen as well as speak. For conflict to have a successful outcome, the conversation has to be two-way. Both parties have to be prepared to understand the other's view. You don't have to agree, but you do have to understand.

"Those who know do not speak. Those who speak do not know."
Lao Tzu

Bruce Tuckman's seminal model of team development proposes that teams typically progress through four stages: Forming, Storming, Norming and Performing. After the initial *forming* stage, when people are polite and focused upon building early relationships, team members will eventually begin to *storm*. The storming process is when members try to exert their influence on issues that affect the team, and is therefore when differences begin to emerge. Whilst the resulting conflicts of opinion can be uncomfortable, Tuckman's model clearly indicates that not only is *storming* predictable and commonplace, it also is essential. Without storming, teams are not able to express what they think and so never truly have the opportunity to put all their cards on the table.

"When two people fully agree, one of them is redundant." Anon

Where an authoritative figure prevents this honest debate, the price paid is a culture of compliance, which is a sure-fire way to mediocrity and high turnover of your best people. Where there is no obvious power structure, the opposite danger is that a culture of *groupthink* will permeate the workplace, in which the desire for conformity and harmony precludes honest opinions being expressed. Both these scenarios stifle individual creativity and contributions, which in turn frustrate those who are willing and able to add value. Groupthink also tends to encourage a sense of righteousness amongst the team, collectively certain that they have it right, reinforced by everybody 'standing together' on the issue. Yet, the situation is far more passive than that; at best, the group are merely 'sitting together', lethargic, unquestioning and bending in unison with the breeze.

Aligning Good People

Graham Hughes, with justifiable pride, declares on his website: "I am, and always will be, the first person to visit every country in the world without flying." Setting off from Argentina on New Year's Day 2009, 201 countries, 160,000 miles, and 1,426 days later he achieved his incredible goal. It was an epic adventure, and you can read about it in his book 'Man of the World'. My interest centred on his many experiences of meeting people around the world, and the goodwill that exists amongst humankind. Hughes comments: "During my four years on the road I met an incredible number of people from, quite literally, every country in the world. Nearly all of them helped me on my way," adding: "you sometimes find that it is those with the very least that give the most."

I was particularly heartened by his experience whilst travelling across Iran. On an overnight bus heading from Shiraz to Khorramshahr, Hughes sensed the old Persian lady sitting in front of him was unsettled. His concern that he might be the cause of her unease, turned to confusion when the old lady reached back and passed him her mobile phone, gesturing for him to put it to his ear. On the other end of the line was her grandson, Seyed, who could speak English. Seyed explained that his grandmother had called him because she was worried that arriving in Khorramshahr at 5 a.m., he would have nowhere to go and nothing to eat. Seyed explained that his grandmother wanted to know if she could take him home with her and give him breakfast! Several hours later, and after enjoying a wonderful breakfast, grandson Seyed arrived and drove Hughes to the port and ensured he caught the ferry to Kuwait. That's a story to restore anybody's faith in humankind! Hughes' website, www.theodysseyexpedition.com, concludes: "Here's to all the incredible people – from every country in the world – who helped make it happen."

My life's experience echoes Hughes', and I hope yours does too, that the vast majority of people we meet are 'good'. And if that is true, it makes sense that conflict can virtually always be resolved. But we need to connect and to talk if we are to achieve that. In the Old Testament, Abraham espoused the virtues of 'neighbourliness', of being welcoming to others, whoever they are. It is a value that every parent seeks to instil in their children and every major religion espouses: 'treat others as you would wish to be treated yourself'. Seyed and his grandmother are shining examples. There is so much more that connects us than separates us, something we can forget in our fractious and often frantic world. All too often we overlook doing 'the right thing', including resolving an incidence of conflict, simply because we are so busy.

This concept was researched during a famous 1973 social experiment undertaken at Princeton Theology Seminary. The experiment focused upon 'social conscience', specifically regarding people's propensity to help others in need, and the results were illuminating. The theology students at the seminary were individually set a task to walk over to a nearby building to give a presentation. The experiment involved two variables; the first was that half of the students were instructed to give a talk on the parable of The Good Samaritan, whilst the other half were to speak on a more general topic. Within each of these two groups, the second variable was that half were told their talk was overdue and they must rush over to the nearby building to give their presentation, whilst the other half were given no indication of time pressure. The researchers then arranged for an actor to be situated between the two buildings, who was to feign feeling unwell as each student passed by. The point of the experiment was to find out how many people would stop to offer help, and which of the two variables had the bigger impact. It turned out that the topic of their talk had minimal influence. Even with heads full of the wonderful Good Samaritan lesson, only 10% of those who had been told to hurry actually stopped to help, compared with around 65% of those who were not under any time pressure. It was therefore each student's perceived time-pressure that most influenced their social conscience; put simply, when we are busy we ignore others, and can fail to do what is clearly the right thing to do. The results should sound a warning bell to us in our busy lives.

Whether our excuse happens to be time constraint, or anything else, the fact is, if we do not make time for others, how can we possibly connect? How can we find that 'third way' referred to by Fisher and Ury in *Getting to Yes*? Leaders who are adept at handling situations where people are in disagreement recognise the importance of putting time aside to address those differences, not by confrontation, but by constructive conversation. For example, walking side-by-side naturally connects people. It neutralises frustrations and creates a friendly atmosphere; no one ever fights walking side-by-side! Holding on to the positive mindset that the vast majority of people are 'good' engenders empathy, with each party respectfully hearing and understanding the other. It is the foundation stone for reaching resolution, and the best leaders do it well.

Avoid assumptions

"If you assume, you make an 'ass' out of 'u' and 'me'" is a well-worn cliché, but well worth repeating. It is so easy to make an assumption about another's position, yet more often than not our assumption will be wrong to some extent or other. A fascinating example emanates from the 1955 United Nations' negotiations,

during the *Cold War*, which were aimed at reducing arms and tension between the Soviet Union and US. Records cite that conflicts arose over America's demands to be allowed to verify underground testing, something the Soviets suspected was in fact an attempt to spy on their broader military capabilities. Whilst some form of moratorium was eventually agreed, those attending the negotiations commented how they felt the reason for the protracted and only-partial resolution was a fundamental misunderstanding over the nature of the inspections. America would have accepted discrete opportunities to check the testing and disarmament progress, yet the Soviets saw it as the Americans having free rein to go wherever they liked. Despite the Cold War being considered the greatest threat to global safety, an incorrect assumption about a straightforward issue derailed much of the progress.

Misunderstandings happen all the time; think how often have you misinterpreted somebody's message, especially when the message isn't delivered face-to-face. Written messages, whether they be carefully constructed emails or on-the-move texts, can be interpreted in so many ways and therefore *misinterpreted* in so many ways! The context and tone of our messages can become so difficult to convey that misunderstandings are inevitable. This is why, within any 'customer complaint' training, the golden rule is to start by asking the customer to explain the situation, and to really probe the full-extent of the issue. Interestingly, there is strong evidence that the process alone of allowing someone to 'get it off their chest' significantly reduces any tension. Listening intently goes a long way to turn a conflict into a conversation, and you haven't actually had to *do* anything! Just showing respect and interest in another's view takes you a long way towards a resolution.

Flex your style, not your muscles

Once you have established a constructive two-way conversation, the remainder of the journey towards *mutual* resolution requires both parties to explore options that each feel would be acceptable, or better still, highly satisfactory. In other words, to achieve a *Win:Win* outcome. This exploration will be steered by two critical factors: the extent to which each party is intent upon optimising *their own position,* versus is prepared to accommodate *the other's position.* These two dimensions are the foundation of the world's most commonly used conflict-handling instrument, the Thomas-Kilmann Instrument (TKI), which is a great resource in developing effective conflict handling strategies. The founders of TKI, Kenneth Thomas and Ralph Kilmann, explored these two dimensions and how placing different levels of importance on each would impact upon conflict-handling strategy, which led them to identify five styles:

1. *It's my way or the highway!* These people are driven to achieve *their* objectives, to 'win the day'. If they have hierarchical power, their approach tends to be: *"Just Do It."* If they don't have power, then their approach will be to push, campaign, cajole or use any other technique they know, to secure the outcome *they* want. We should not automatically dismiss this as a negative style; there are times when it is absolutely appropriate to hold a firm stance, to have a clear point of view and not waiver. If an issue is critically important to you or you feel someone is taking advantage, or you need to take rapid action, it is better to state this assertively and to seek the other person's agreement. However, be careful of over-using this style, unless you want to be seen as arrogant or bullying and, consequently, be left surrounded by 'yes people' who merely follow your orders and add little value.

2. *Have it your way!* These people either don't have a strong view on the issue at hand, or are disinclined to state it. That may be because they feel they do not have the power to fight their case and so would prefer to keep the peace, or because they are prepared to subordinate their views and support your preference on this occasion. Far from revealing weakness, said appropriately, this approach can pay dividends in terms of building relationships, demonstrating reasonableness and trust and enabling others to learn for themselves. If the issue genuinely isn't so important to you, why not accommodate the other person? Doing so most probably strengthens your hand when

next there is disagreement about an issue that *is* important to you. In effect, you are choosing to 'concede the battle to win the war'. However, if you over-use this style, you risk being seen as submissive, having no clear opinions, or being someone who lacks the courage of their convictions. As such, you become the 'willing horse', and don't be surprised when you keep getting flogged.

3. *I'll meet you half way!* These people are notably expedient and achieve this by showing a willingness to 'give and take' in order to resolve conflicts quickly. It works well in non-critical situations, where there is an obvious deal to be struck, and where both parties have equal power and influence. Classic 'wheeler dealers' make their living in this territory. Indeed, I hear stories of markets abroad where traders genuinely are disappointed if you don't haggle and will even insist that you do. I have to say though, on all my travels, I've yet to find anyone offended by me paying full price! Regardless, if you over-use this compromise approach it can lead to a lack of trust, because people know your position always contains built-in 'haggling room', which implies that your initial proposals are never a good deal. As a consequence, people learn simply to counter your approach in the opposite direction. As a result, life becomes a 'tit for tat' negotiation, always trying to meet at a favourable point between two unrealistic positions. Because each party has to compromise their position, each is left feeling only moderately happy with the outcome.

4. *Leave well alone!* We all will recognise moments when we have opted to 'put our heads in the sand' to avoid a conflict situation, neither supporting nor disagreeing with the other person. Whilst this may seem like an evasive strategy or perhaps even a 'non-strategy', actually it is a very valid approach in certain circumstances. For example, if the issue is trivial, if you are extremely busy, if the other person simply drains you by wanting to debate every single issue, or if the conflict is untimely or even dangerous in some way, then it might be entirely appropriate to step back and leave well alone. There may also be times when you know that other factors are in play, for example the other person is having a really difficult time, and your wisdom tells you to just let it go. That said, if you over-use this

approach and consistently ignore issues, you will come across as uninterested, disengaged or even dismissive, in which case all those ignored issues simply accumulate and fester.

5. *Let's find a Win:Win!* This type of approach, sometimes called the 'problem solving' approach, involves a lot of thought and creativity in searching for a solution with which both parties genuinely are happy. It requires commitment from both sides to have an open and constructive conversation. Both parties need to fully understand each other's position and be prepared to be innovative and explore new territory to find the optimal solution. The approach brings obvious benefits, including 'better' solutions, and therefore greater shared commitment and much closer relationships. It may sound the ideal approach to conflict. However, it too can be over-used. At times, when the issue at hand does not warrant this level of time and effort, it can create work overload or frustrations if an extensive process has to be followed for *every* issue. Also, it only makes sense to adopt this mutual approach if the other party has similar intentions. *Win:Win* only works when it's a two-way street; so you have to establish accurately the other person's intentions, most notably whether they have any interest in you also reaching a highly satisfactory outcome.

⚜ Reflection Point:

What we learn from the different conflict-handling styles is that each has its rightful place and when used appropriately will result in the optimal outcome. Equally, if we over-use any of the styles, we are likely to make a poor impression. Therefore, the challenge for a leader is to have the flexibility to recognise and adapt to each conflict situation, using good judgement to select the best approach. 'One trick ponies' will no doubt have some successes but will have many more failures. Most people have one or two preferred, or 'default', styles that they naturally adopt in conflict situations, so reflect on how you most commonly approach conflict. Do you lean too heavily on one or two? Do you have any 'blind spots' i.e. approaches that you hardly ever use? If so, how could you vary your approach more? As ever, seeking feedback from others will provide insights you simply will not get from self-reflection.

Don't just say "No"

There will be times when, despite best efforts, a resolution to the conflict simply cannot be found. At that point, a leader has the authority and a duty to say "No". It is not an easy message to give, but it doesn't serve anybody well to duck those moments. You have to be honest and courageous, and in response you can expect to hear a whole range of negative emotions, from mild disappointment to total dismay.

But there is a way to mitigate these responses, a way to demonstrate the wider picture and to soften the blow. To reach a reasonably positive, or at least accepting, outcome requires a four-stage approach:

1. **Empathise.** Everybody's point of view is valid and should be respected. Rarely is any viewpoint entirely wrong, nor for that matter entirely correct. We should take the time to understand the other person's view, and let them know we do. It is appropriate and helpful to reflect back that we understand their view and even to endorse any elements of their proposal with which we agree.

2. **Give your Reasons** why you have a different opinion. If the reality is that you do not agree with their request, you owe an explanation, and because you have been empathetic, it usually will encourage reciprocation. Be careful how many reasons you give for your disagreement. The theory of 'argument distillation' offers a powerful insight here, proposing that we should distil our rationale down to a small number of key points. Doing so helps keep a clear focus on the main points and avoids people switching off or feeling overwhelmed. Additionally, if you do include minor or weak points in your argument, do so recognising that they will be the hardest for you to defend, yet will the first attacked and will psychologically undermine your stronger points.

3. **Say "No".** Having explained your key reasons, you have to deliver the 'No', and deliver it unambiguously. That said, be considerate and say it with empathy; it is only right to demonstrate that you genuinely are sorry to disappoint.

4. **Emphasise** what you *are* willing to agree to. This might be to support part of their request, or to revisit the decision at an agreed future point, or to compromise in other areas. Try to leave the discussion on a positive note; virtually every situation offers that option.

Life would be dull if we agreed all of the time, so we should embrace conflict as a natural part of our vibrant lives, necessary for creativity to flourish, the proverbial 'grit in the oyster' without which we would not have pearls. When conflict does arise, we should approach it with an open and constructive mind, varying our style to increase the likelihood of a positive outcome. On those occasions when resolution simply can't be reached, handle the impasse without defensiveness, say 'No' in the right way, and leave others able to move forward with relationships intact.

11/10

Allocating Time

The feeling of 'spinning plates', and lots of them, is commonplace in today's high-speed world. The most frequent response to our common greeting: "How's things?" must surely be either "Fine, thanks." or "Busy!" By "Fine, thanks" we mean "I'm too busy to tell you more" or "I recognise you're too busy to hear more!" Modern working lives are highly pressured, and we juggle those demands with our family commitments and social activities. Adding to that, the information at our disposal these days is effectively infinite.

As long ago as 1991, Richard Saul Wurman's groundbreaking book *Information Anxiety* warned that: "the information explosion has backfired, leaving us inundated with facts but starved of understanding". Fast forward to 2017, and data specialist Bernard Marr estimates: "Every two days, we create as much data as we did from the beginning of time until 2003", and further predicts that data quantities will increase ten-fold in the next three years. With all that 'noise' competing for our attention, and with so many plates to spin, it is no surprise that many people experience a 'time famine'.

Do you ever stop to think whether you are spinning the right plates, and whether you are spinning too many? Your reflection should include also whether you are being selective enough about the information you attend to. In short, do you utilise your time well?

"If you want to know your past - look into your present conditions. If you want to know your future - look into your present actions." Chinese Proverb

Our family calendar last year had a page that struck a chord with me. The illustration for the month of December contained the following phrases: 'There is no such thing as free time'. 'There is no such thing as spare time'. 'There is no such thing as quality time'. 'There is no such thing as down time'. 'There is no such thing as the wrong time'. 'There is no such thing as the right time'. The concluding statement was: "THERE IS ONLY TIME."

It is such an important message. Life apportions many resources unfairly; some are born to wealth, others to poverty; some are born in good health, others with illness or disability etc. We all start from our own unique starting point. Time, however, is not unique: time is the great leveller. We all have the identical amount - 168 hours per week - and what we do with it determines everything else. We can spend three hours watching TV, surfing the web or gaming, or alternatively we could reduce that to two hours and learn a foreign language for one hour - a simple switch with a big impact. Try reducing to one hour, and replace with one hour playing a family game and one hour doing professional studies - another big impact. Others will spend all their three hours supporting a local charity - a huge impact! Be honest, how much time do you spending in front of your TV, PC or multitude of devices? We even have TV shows watching people watching TV! Let's not blame TV or any other media or entertainment options we have available, all of which can be great additions to our lives; that is, as long as *they* serve *us*, and not *vice versa*. I simply want to emphasise how many 'time stealers' are out there, and whichever may be 'stealing' your precious time, if you considered the whole picture of how you allocate your time, would you choose to make changes? I bet we *all* would.

There are no Pause or Rewind buttons in life. When time's gone, it's gone. So what you do with your finite time deserves proper consideration. The phrase 'time management' is an oxymoron; you cannot 'manage' time. Time 'happens'; you can't speed it or slow it (let's not get into the Theory of Relativity!). All you *can* do is manage your activities, and so the central issue is how you allocate your time i.e. your *prioritisation*. We can't always be productive, because our bodies and minds need to rest. Watching trash TV or lounging around is not all bad; we all need those zone -out moments. Yet we do have to be mindful about how much of our precious time they consume.

"The past cannot be regained, although we can learn from it; the future is not yet ours even though we must plan for it. Time is now; we have only today." Charles Hummell

Overcome Inertia, Get Going

Here's a question for you: *"Five birds are sitting on a telephone wire, and two decide to fly south. How many are left?"*

Most people answer: *'Three'* for obvious reasons, but actually all five are left. You see, 'deciding to fly' isn't the same as 'flying'. For those two birds actually to fly south requires them to stop deciding and start flapping. It's the story of our lives; too often we are full of good intentions, yet we don't translate them into actions. Our intentions don't take us towards our goals: our *actions* do. Too often, we 'talk a good talk' but don't 'walk a good walk'.

"In a world full of people, only some want to fly. Isn't that crazy!" Seal (lyrics from *'Crazy'*)

Every single one of your achievements started when you overcame some form of inertia, became clear about the direction in which you wanted to move, and then got moving. Few examples of 'walking the walk' – literally in this case - can be more inspiring than that of Legson Kayira, as recounted in his autobiography *I Will Try*.

Legson was born in Malawi in the early 1940's, within an impoverished family. Indeed, soon after his birth, unable to feed him, his mother reputedly threw him into the local river.

Thankfully, Legson was rescued and went on to receive a schooling. His secondary school in Livingstonia had the motto 'I Will Try', which became the title of his autobiography. It was from there that sixteen-year-old Legson set off on a remarkable journey to fulfil his dream to study for a degree at a US college. His only option was to go by foot!

With hardly any possessions to his name, sleeping alone outdoors, foraging for food and barely surviving, he nevertheless kept going, working when he could for a small pay and encountering strangers who gave a little of what they had to help him on his way. 2,000 km and over a year later, he reached Kampala, Uganda, but he remained a world-away from his dream. In fact, his walk had not even reached half-way. Over the next months he settled in Kampala to recuperate and earn a little money to continue his journey. During that time, Legson would spend as much time as possible in the library where he came upon the US Information Service Directory and, in particular, information regarding the Skagit Valley College in Washington State. Without delay, he wrote to the Dean, explaining his quest to study there and his journey so far. So impressed was the Dean, he replied offering not only a scholarship but also a job to support himself whilst there.

Buoyed by this incredible offer, Legson then set off for the next leg of his journey, a 2,500 km walk to Khartoum, Egypt, where he planned to work until he could afford a flight to the US. By the time he arrived in Khartoum, news of his incredible journey had been spread amongst Skagit Valley's students, and a collection had been made to pay for Legson's airfare. Using the last of his savings to buy a pair of shoes, he arrived overjoyed, more than two years after setting out on his incredible journey.

The moral of Legson's story is reflected well by Conrad Hilton's observation: *"Success seems to be connected with action. Successful people keep moving. They make mistakes but they never quit."* Legson undoubtedly was a very talented man, but regardless of talent, it is a person's effort and perseverance that counts for so much. The Roman proverb, *Initium est dimidium facti* means 'the beginning is half of the deed' and serves to remind us how important it is to overcome inertia and get started. Once we have momentum, continuing towards our goals becomes easier than giving up!

"The start is what stops most people." Don Shula, NFL Coach

Actions speak louder than words

'Waiting' is a trap we all fall into. Waiting for conditions to be just right before we set off, waiting for blockers to fall away, waiting for others to join us, waiting for permission and waiting, well, for the sake of waiting! Ryan Holiday writes in his book *Ego is the Enemy* about the importance of taking action, observing: *"Talking* and *doing* fight for the same resources."* He goes on to share Robert Greene's concept of 'Alive Time or Dead Time': "dead time, when people are passive and waiting, and alive time, when people are learning and acting and utilizing every second." It is a useful concept for leaders to apply when analysing how they, and others, are utilising their time.

We should recognise the importance of balance at this point. A 'hamster wheel' is a very effective device to optimise 'alive time', and also to leave people burnt-out! 'All things in moderation' we are often told, and there is a healthy truth to that. I definitely don't advocate sustained long working hours. More often than not, long hours reflect a culture of *'presenteeism'*, where being present trumps being productive. At other times, they reflect inadequate resourcing, or unreasonable management. Yet none of these causes are sustainable, and it is the best people who pack their bags first.

However, let's be realistic, rather like the old saying: 'if you want something done, give it to a busy person', there invariably *is* a close correlation between levels of ambition and working hours. The role of a leader is to engender enthusiasm in others to raise their aim, so they have a focus and determination to commit to their work. Best-selling author John Grisham reputedly would start writing at 05.30 each morning so that he could complete at least one page of his latest book before heading off to his job as a lawyer. Similarly, scriptwriter and novelist Greg Evans put it: *"I do not have superior intelligence or faultless looks. I only succeeded because I was still working after everyone else went to sleep."*

"Leaders must be up front, up to date, up to their job, and up early in the morning." Lord Sieff, M&S Chairman 1972 - 84

He Who Shouts the Loudest

The contrast between work that is 'important', and that which is 'urgent', dates back at least to the middle of the last century. US President Eisenhower referred to it: *"I have two kinds of problems, the urgent and the important. The urgent are not important, and the important are not urgent."* These dual factors are unlikely to be as mutually exclusive as Eisenhower suggests; many 'urgent' tasks are also 'important', and *vice versa*. Nonetheless, urgency and importance unquestionably are the dominant drivers that influence how we allocate our time. It was Stephen Covey who eventually brought Eisenhower's thinking into the mainstream, through his bestseller *The 7 Habits of Highly Effective People*. He developed the well-known 'time management grid', shown below:

	Urgent	Not Urgent
Important	**1** Just do it!	**2** Game Changers
Not Important	**3** Time Stealers	**4** Leave it!

Allocating our time intelligently across the quadrants will determine our productivity and performance. However, the problem is that urgent tasks 'shout the loudest'. For example, phones demand to be answered, emails responded to, visitors welcomed, complaints handled, project deadlines met etc. These urgent tasks are all legitimate and all require an allocation of our finite time; but it is essential to realise that they are almost exclusively driven by others. We are rarely in control when all we do is react to the 'urgent' demands of others.

Covey's grid provides a great discussion framework for leaders to share with colleagues. Allocating whatever time is necessary to tasks that fall under Quadrant 1 is a 'no brainer'. So too is allocating as little time as possible to tasks within Quadrant 4. What is most telling though, in terms of identifying high performers, is how people allocate their remaining time between Quadrants 2 and 3. Some people lean towards the 'reactive' Quadrant 3, prioritising 'urgent but not important' tasks. However, those who are seen as high performers, lean more frequently towards the 'proactive' Quadrant 2, focusing on the 'important but not urgent' tasks. Those tasks demand far greater proactivity because they are self-initiated and have a longer-term focus. This quadrant belongs to the self-starters, and they recognise and reach their longer-term goals!

Time allocation across the quadrants clearly will depend upon the specific role in question. Whilst, for example, scientific researchers will most probably allocate a huge proportion of their time to 'important' work, a paramedic's life will be dominated by the 'urgency' of daily crises. That said, to be truly effective, the paramedic needs also to consider 'important' tasks. For example, undertaking broader professional development may not save a life today but most probably will save many over a career. If you are entirely reactive, your life will be dominated by the urgency of others' demands, and you may never make adequate time to think about the future and plan ahead. The long-term impact of short-term thinking can be disastrous, just as the rewards of taking a long term view and developing skills for the future can be enormous.

"If you want 1 year of prosperity, grow grain. If you want 10 years of prosperity, grow trees. If you want 100 years of prosperity, grow people." Chinese proverb

Consider the long-term planning that went into the use of the longbow, a game-changing weapon in medieval warfare. Laws stipulating compulsory archery practice from boyhood date back to at least the 13th century and had a huge influence on the outcome of many battles. Perhaps most famous was the Battle of Agincourt in 1415, when an army of 6,000 men comprising over 5,000 longbow archers, led by Henry V[th], gained victory over an army of over 20,000 well-equipped and battle-ready troops. Skilled usage of the longbow, which was almost 2 metres in length, required exceptional arm and hand strength, together with an ability to fully distend the shoulder joint. It was only through long-term practice from childhood that this combination of strength and flexibility could be developed in order to make use of the weapon's devastating power, accuracy and range. Indeed, the demands upon the body of such intense training remain clearly evident to archeologists today. Male skeletons from that era reveal enlarged, hyper-flexed or irregular bone growth in the shoulders, arms, hands and right fingers. The legal requirement to practise every day from the age of twelve came at a high cost but, in the hands of a skilled archer, arrows could be shot twice as far, ten times more frequently, and still more accurately than by any crossbow. The longbow, and the long-term training regimes it demanded, transformed medieval warfare.

Beware the 'Turn-Uppers'

Every leader must consider where amongst their team to allocate their finite time. Take a look at the model opposite, which reflects a common proportionate breakdown of a team.

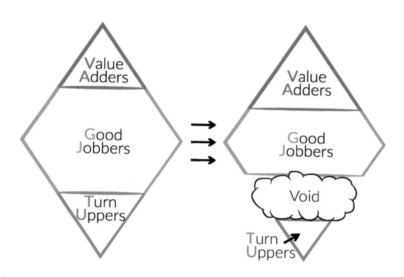

Within the team there will be some members at the top of the diamond, usually 10-20%, who we categorise as 'Value Adders'. These are the people who are proactive, positive and professional, and who push boundaries in their personal development, and go the extra mile in their role. Being self-motivated, they have a limited need to feed off your or anybody else's energy; more commonly they are 'radiators', not 'drains'. Smart leaders avoid micro-management with these people, ensuring they receive the appropriate recognition and reward for their excellent contribution, and look for any opportunity for them to infect others with their positive attitude.

At the bottom of the diamond, again usually comprising around 10-20% of the team, are the 'Turn Uppers', those people who show up for work but do only what is necessary to get by and stay in employment. They begrudge doing anything beyond their role definition, and if they are committed to anything it is to 'work to rule. Businesses saddled with these people can survive only if they operate in a 'low or no' competition environment, or if there are sufficient committed team members whose efforts counter-balance their shortcomings. Regrettably, some 'turn uppers' go further, and actually act as detractors of performance; they get their kicks from draining colleagues' enthusiasm and sabotaging performance. Leaders need to have a short-fuse with these types; everybody deserves a chance, but if it is not taken, and taken quickly, then every door should lead to the 'Exit'!

The middle section is where we find the 'Good Jobbers', who proportionately make up the majority of team members, at around 60%-80%. These people typically can be relied upon to do a good job, although are unlikely to utilise their talents fully and rarely will go the extra mile. Leaders should focus heavily upon these people, not only because they form the majority, but also because many of them can be influenced up the scale, often without huge incentive. Also, as they move further upwards, they move away from the 'turn uppers', creating a void in the lower part of the diamond shape, and as a result are less likely to get dragged down in that direction.

Research organisation Gallup routinely track employee engagement levels, and it is interesting that figures from their global surveys are largely consistent with the above, concluding across many years of research that only around 15% of employees are 'actively engaged' (meaning they show genuine enthusiasm and commitment, are proactive in offering support, and can be relied upon to go the extra mile), around 25% of respondents are 'actively disengaged' (indicating they are both unhappy and unproductive at work), and the remaining 60% are 'not engaged' (meaning they are unlikely to offer significant discretionary effort).

Transactional – Facilitative - Generative

Regardless of a person's job, whether a blacksmith, a brain surgeon or *your* job, everybody allocates their time across three categories of work: Transactional, Facilitative and Generative.

- *Transactional* activities relate to you doing your job and producing your own output. Regardless of whether the work is highly complex or menial, the key point is '*you* are doing the doing'.

- *Facilitative* activity relates to you enabling others to do their job so they produce their own output. Whether you are leading, managing, directing, motivating or instructing, the key point is you are adopting whatever approach you consider most appropriate to ensure '*others* do the doing'.

- *Generative* activity relates to you stepping back and thinking about new ideas and future direction. You may be daydreaming, brainstorming, strategising, networking or researching, but the key point is 'you are *thinking*, not doing'.

Each category of work plays an important part in every role, so the challenge for everyone is to get the balance right between the three. It is invaluable for leaders to reflect on how they allocate their time and whether they feel they should make some adjustments. One of the best pieces of feedback I ever received was from a colleague who observed: "I never see you looking out of the window." It was a very insightful point, delivered with his characteristic warmth and emotional intelligence. What he was saying was: "You're always too busy *doing*" and, by implication: "you don't spend enough time *thinking*." When we become too busy spinning plates, we change from human-beings, to human-doings. He was right; I needed to raise my 'generative' game!

The tables overleaf offers insights into the benefits of getting your time allocation about right, and the pitfalls of focusing too much or too little time in any of the categories:

Transactional		
About Right	**Too much**	**Too little**
You're a role model You are admired for your effort, contribution and specialist skills, and for not just dumping work on everyone else.	*You're not a leader* You are known as a hard worker, but people wonder *why* you are the leader! You might as well pass that role on to someone else.	*You're not admired* You are 'Mr/Mrs Tefal', everything sliding off your desk. People don't learn from you because you don't produce anything.

Facilitative		
About Right	**Too much**	**Too little**
You're an enabler You know how to engage and enable, judging people's level of 'will and skill', and providing the type of support they need.	*You're not a worker* Whilst people may appreciate your support, they can also feel smothered or overloaded, and would appreciate seeing *you* do something!	*You're not connected* People feel 'lost' on this sort of team, not getting the direction or support needed. Only resilient and experienced members can cope.

Generative		
About Right	**Too much**	**Too little**
You're a visionary You reassure people, as a strategic leader who demonstrates vision and establishes the direction the team should move in.	*You're not visible* "Where is he?" "Not sure, but I think I saw his head in the clouds!" is the team's chatter. There comes a point when ideas have to be actioned, and you've gone past that point!	*You're not informed* You fall into the trap of the 'busy fool', spinning every plate thrown in your direction. As seafarers say: *"If you don't know where you're going, any wind will do."*

🌙 Action Point:

elf-perception so often is self-deception because our eyes look
utwards, and that makes it difficult to judge ourselves. Share
his model with trusted colleagues, and ask them how they
erceive you allocate your time, and what adjustments they think
vould be effective. Reflect on the feedback and ensure you make
he desired adjustments, and then check back in with those
olleagues for their validation that you have changed.

pinning plates

Much of our lives is governed by the 'need for speed'. We fill
very moment and, worse still, we multi-task through every
noment. On-line learning systems are currently being introduced
hat recognise when we have just seconds of down-time on our
omputers; for example, waiting for an email to send will trigger
a piece of learning to flash up on our screens. Instead of a
noment of mental pause, a brief respite for the brain, we will be
nformed: "The French for *shirt* is *chemise*." or "The capital of
Mongolia is Ulaanbaatar." Before long, we'll all know everything
and will be exhausted too! A prominent US magazine editor wrote
ecently about how she runs on a treadmill in her office to keep
it whilst simultaneously working. At home she watches TV on
ast forward to cram more in. It's impressive at one level.
However, it seems we don't pay very much attention to very
nuch anymore; we are just crazy busy, being crazy busy. Jim
Rohn commented: *"I find it fascinating that most people plan
their vacations with better care than they plan their lives.
Perhaps that is because escape is easier than change."* It is a
challenge worth reflecting on, although I suspect it is 'busy-ness',
not escape, that is the real issue.

*"Vision without action is a daydream, action without vision is a
nightmare."* Japanese adage

Generative' thinkers, however, are different, at least some of
the time. Somehow, they find a way of escaping the deluge of
distractions out there, and find the headspace to think about the

bigger picture - the strategic factors that determine the longer term outcomes. First, they take time to reflect back and review events. As Olympic gold-medalist Kriss Akabusi put it: *"The past is for reference,"* although please note he also added: *"but not for residence!"* Generative thinkers also think ahead to prepare for where they want to get to. You cannot throw yourself wholeheartedly at a task until you know what you are aiming at. Think of the typical change you see in someone who likes jogging but who then decides to enter a major sponsored event. Observe how their routines and discipline change from that 'moment of clarity' onwards. Similarly, think about any jigsaw puzzle you might buy; what invariably is on the top of the box? It is the 'big picture', the end-goal you're trying to achieve, and it would take many times longer to complete the puzzle if you didn't have that picture, the 'vision', to aim for.

It is the generative thinkers in life who help us shift away from constant fire-fighting, helping to formulate and visualise our end goals. As leaders, we need to encourage colleagues to apply more thinking within their roles.

Action Point:

Consider to what extent you and your team actually stop to reflect on your performance. Do you consciously review significant experiences, and explore what can be learned from it. Ensuring that you create space for you and your team to both *'look back and reflect'* and *'look forward and plan'* is an essential part of your leadership role.

Habits: Helping or Hindering?

Habits are essential for life because we have neither the mental bandwidth nor the time to consider afresh how we should approach every daily task. As a result, habits dominate the vast majority of our actions and thoughts.

The so-called 'pike syndrome' refers to an experiment with this famously predatory fish, which illustrates just how much habits can limit us. If you put a pike in a tank together with a handful of minnows, the pike will watch them for a while and before long it will attack and eat them. If, instead, you put a sheet of clear glass in the tank, with the pike on one side and the minnows on the other, the pike will try to reach the minnows and will continue to try to do so, colliding with the glass for several hours before eventually giving up. But the really interesting thing is, if you then remove the glass, the minnows will all swim safely around and the pike, now conditioned not to attack, will starve to death!

Habits, invariably, are sub-conscious, so we quickly become accustomed to do them repeatedly. Just like the pike, every day we simply fail to recognise and take advantage of what is out there right in front of us. Habits are self-reinforcing and become hard-wired in our brains, leading us into both virtuous and vicious circles of behaviour. Regardless of whether our habits are good or bad, what we must recognise is that, as Aristotle famously put it: *"We are what we repeatedly do."* It pays to be aware of your habits and to reflect upon which ones are helpful and which may be hindering. Honest self-reflection and an enthusiastic appetite for feedback will get you a very long way to understanding and adapting your habits.

Action point:

What we do with our 168 hours per week will define the outcome of our lives; it is as simple and significant as that. I am not suggesting you become overly-stressed about time; that's not helpful. However, if you want to 'get on' in life you need to 'get on' with whatever will get you there!

So here're a few points that you may want to reflect upon:

• Be careful that *Urgent* tasks aren't eating too many of your hours.

- Be careful that *Important* tasks aren't eating too few of you hours!

- Use a *'To Do'* list. It will help you get started and keep distractions at bay.

- Confront *Blockers*. "Three steps forward & two steps back" eat valuable time.

- Check your *Habits,* and be honest about whether they serve you well.

- Visualise your *End Goal*. As Stephen Covey's *Habit of Highly Effective People #2* puts it: *"Begin with the end in mind."*

Section 4:
The Mark of a Leader

Chapters:

12. Empathy

13. Authenticity

14. Right level of Pressure

15. Resilience

Empathy 12

"Before you criticise another person, walk a mile in their shoes", we are often told. There is a humorous extension, which goes: "and that way, when you do criticise them, you're a mile away and you've got their shoes!" Let's ignore that humorous bit because there is a serious point here. The metaphor clearly implies that empathy goes beyond knowing facts about or the opinions of another. It is about being able to experience how someone *feels* about something, genuinely sensing what they are sensing. This leads to a far deeper and intimate understanding. Few people fully appreciate this, and even fewer actually take the time to truly empathise.

In preparation for attending a festival of Wagner operas a Bayreuth in 1884, French composer Gabriel Fauré advised a friend to: "take loads of handkerchiefs because you will cry a great deal." And he continued: "Also take a sedative because you will be exalted to the point of delirium!" Around the same time the London Musical World was commenting that Wagner "inspire. the most appalling tedium", adding: "We should prefer a state of perpetual coma". What on earth was going on with such wildly different reviews? And who should we believe?

Such bewilderingly wide-ranging views are the familiar norm amongst any customer review forums. Scrolling down Trip Adviso reviews, I am just about to click 'Book' as I read reviews from guests who loved the impeccable hotel with its outstanding staff when I stumble upon the first of many accounts of dirty bed linen, draughty windows, lukewarm food, and surly staff. Bette restart the search! The same happens whenever I want to buy anything; customer feedback ratings are spread across a huge spectrum. Some of the differences will of course reflec' genuinely different experiences. Maybe the hotel was short staffed that time, or maybe somebody simply made an error and was denied the opportunity to rectify it. However, what you cannot escape is the reality that across all walks of life people have wide-ranging views, and they reflect honest opinion.

This gives us a great insight into the concept and importance o empathy. It is wrong and pointless to reject another person': view, but it is invaluable to seek to understand it. To lister intently to someone has a profound effect on our understanding of them and on the relationship you have with them. Plato implored us to: *"Be kinder than necessary, for everyone you mee is fighting some kind of battle,"* and it is only through empathy that we learn of others' battles.

Returning to the 'shoe' analogy, and extending it, remember tha before you can step into another's shoes you must first take you own off. For many people, that is the tougher side of developing empathy; they can discipline themselves to listen to others opinions, but they cannot suspend their own. If you *can* do that it means you extend your awareness that everyone is unique, and hey will have a unique perspective. Recognising that this is at he heart of embracing diversity creates a massive advantage vhen it comes to connecting and engaging with the seven billion ndividuals on our planet.

Empathy is in decline

Ve live in a world that is vastly more complex, mobile and fast-)aced than previous generations ever encountered. Our ncreasingly tech-savvy populations use social media to interact :onstantly with their legions of 'friends'. When not consumed by ill this 'socialising', we are immersed in the ever more :ompetitive and demanding workplace. The only respite we know s to sit at our PCs playing computer games or flop in front of our "Vs watching reality stars share their unreal lives. This is not a vorld that encourages us to take the time to get to know .omeone well. We don't have, or more to the point don't *make*, ime to do this. Our experience of truly 'being there' for others is :roding rapidly.

There is much research to evidence this deterioration in levels of :mpathy, including a major study in 2017 by the University of Michigan that analysed the attitudes and behaviours of 14,000 .tudents over a 30-year period. The researchers wanted to know 10w frequently students, for example, "tried to understand their riends' perspectives", or "felt concern for less fortunate)eople". The results were not reassuring, revealing an estimated 10% drop in empathy levels over the period 1979-2009, and ndicating that rate of decline was most notable from around !000 onwards. With all we know about our societies, it seems ikely that the decline in levels of empathy will have continued .ince that study.

There is always a silver lining to these types of clouds, and that is f you can remain within the declining number of people who *are* :mpathetic, your leadership will be even more positively dif](differentiated. If we reflect back upon some of the key eadership themes we have covered, being empathetic has to "aise our ability to inspire, to co-create, to demonstrate individual consideration, to build trusting relationships, and to gain commitment. Whilst it seems irrefutable from all the research that empathy levels are in decline, *you* can be a part of the movement to turn that tide, and your leadership capability will soar as a result.

Socrates agrees

Educationalists use the term *'Socratic method'* to describe a learning methodology that engages others in cooperative but critical debate. Part of the genius of Socrates was his acknowledgement that a greater genius lay in the collective minds of all his students (well, one of them was Plato!), and so he would 'teach' his students by engaging them in debate. Rather than Socrates seeking to share his own wisdom, the Socratic method, also known as *maieutics* (meaning 'midwife'), sought to give birth to new ideas. Those new ideas invariably came not from Socrates, but from his students.

This ability and willingness to explore others' thoughts sits at the heart of what it means to be empathetic - to find out what is going through another person's head. Socrates extended this insight to understand the process of how people are influenced. Let's start at the end, with Socrates' conclusion that a person's logical argument is but the final step, of three steps, that you can use to influence other people. Rarely is it effective to rely solely upon a logical argument, however robust you think it is. How many times, for example, have you thought: *"Are they ever going to 'get' this, I've explained it ten times already!"* or *"They cannot be listening; this is a no-brainer."* If you have parented teenagers, how many times have you presented perfect logic, only for it to be dismissed out of hand? Well, the problem always comes back to one conclusion; it may be a perfectly logical case, but it is only 'perfect' to *you*! Within the field of Sales, it is well recognised that: "People buy on emotion and justify by logic." In other words, most often, our 'heart' quickly decides what we would like to have, such as: "I really fancy the steak on the menu", or "I'd really like to try Costa Rica for our next holiday."

From that point, our brains simply need to find whatever logic might reinforce that decision. The world is full of data, and our brains are powerful, and so we are very adept at finding the rationale we need. If Logic really is the *final* step, and additionally may be more-or-less governed by 'emotional' decisions anyway, then we should focus a lot of attention upon what Socrates suggests are the two preceding steps.

The first is to establish your Credibility, not just in general terms, but also in connection with the specific issue you are seeking to influence. Sometimes credibility is clear-cut; if a medical consultant prescribes three 'xyz' tablets a day to be taken for two weeks, you are unlikely to say: "How's about I take some 'abc' tablets instead, just for one week?" The credibility of the doctor's 'white coat' seals the deal. For most of us however, our credibility takes a while to establish, whilst we build our rapport and relationship, provide good advice, prove ourselves knowledgeable and reliable in what we deliver, show integrity in our dealings etc. Whatever the situation, and however long it takes, our credibility is an essential foundation stone. Where we lack credibility, our efforts to influence others will almost certainly flounder. Let us assume for now that we have been successful in building sufficient credibility, and move on with Socrates' model.

That second step is to build Empathy with the person you are seeking to influence. Empathetic people demonstrate one skill, or you might consider it a trait, noticeably better than others; they *really* listen, by which I mean they don't just hear the words. Instead, they listen deeply to what is being said, probing and enquiring, and paying full attention. This depth of listening is uncommon, and people rarely mistake it when they encounter it. In any relationship, the greatest respect you can show is to truly want to listen and understand. The resulting empathy builds the strongest bonds, which are the ideal platform for influencing.

Empathy has an even more tangible impact; now that you know exactly how the other person feels about an issue, you are ideally placed to put forward the logical case that is 'perfect' for *them*. Without that insight, as author and sales consultant Mahan Khalsa puts it: *"The less we truly understand our stakeholders the larger the proposal of solution will be, in the hope that one element of it might actually be the thing they want or need."* On the contrary, empathetic people gain the insights that enable them to hit the nail on the head, every time.

Careful, you might even fall in love

One of the most watched TED Talks of 2015 came from Mandy Len Catron, with her talk *Falling in love is the easy part*. A 1997 psychology study of 'interpersonal closeness' had triggered Catron's interest, notably the suggestion that mutual openness, and therefore vulnerability, fostered closeness and strengthened relationships. To test this, Catron proposed a set of 36 questions of gradually increasing intimacy, that couples who might be seeking a romantic connection should ask each other. Each of the partners would, in turn, listen intently to the other's answer. Early questions in the sequence include things like: *"Whom would you want as a dinner guest?"* and *"Would you like to be famous? In what way?"* Towards the end of the sequence the intimacy dial has been turned right up to questions such as: *"When did you last cry in front of another person?"* and *"Share a personal problem, and ask your partner's advice."*

The results, cue the drum roll, were a resounding success! Love did indeed seem to develop more frequently when Catron's questioning process was followed. Indeed, not only can you watch the TED talk and read the article, you can now even get the App providing you with the necessary fail-safe tools to find love. The impact of taking time to truly understand another and build deep empathy could not be more convincingly proven. Albert Einstein noted: *"Gravitation is not responsible for people falling in love."* He was right; it seems that Empathy *is*.

🕯️ Action Point:

Michael Bungay Stanier's excellent book, *The Coaching Habit*, promotes the idea that a great way to start a coaching conversation is simply to ask: *"What's on your mind?"* Such an informal and open question puts the coach in a great place to build empathy, and the biggest challenge then becomes to 'zip up', and 'listen up' to the full answer. Resolve to use that question far more frequently.

If you are not familiar with British TV comedies, you may not recognise the cartoon picture of 'Del Boy', one of the UK's most-loved comedy characters. Despite having a heart of gold, he is nonetheless always up to some sort of dodgy money-making scheme. If you buy something from Del Boy you can be sure it is 100% fake!

Good leadership, of course, is the total opposite; it has to be authentic. Socrates' maxim: "Know Thyself" has served for millennia as a clear reminder to all leaders to ensure they have a high level of self-awareness. Beyond that, leaders must constantly ensure they remain true to who they are. When we know what a person stands for, and know that they will be consistent in demonstrating that and will hold themselves to account for doing so, we respect and admire that person.

The career of Edmond Locard (1877-1966) was very bad news for the criminal fraternity. Having studied medicine and law, Locard decided upon taking the role as assistant to a leading criminologist and in 1910 succeeded in becoming the director of what is believed to be the first ever crime laboratory, based in an attic in Lyon, France. From his laboratory, Locard became a pioneer in the field of forensic science, his ground-breaking 'Exchange Principle' asserting that: "With contact between two items, there will be an exchange." In other words: "Every contact leaves a trace." Locard explained: "Wherever he steps, whatever he touches, whatever he leaves, even unconsciously, will serve as a silent witness against him."

Locard's 'principle' can be extended to help explain the way in which leaders make an impact and the extent of that impact. Only very occasionally do we make an impact through magnanimous gestures. Instead, the impact we make happens as a consequence of our countless small actions and interactions. Few examples can have more dramatic consequences than businessman Gerald Ratner's comment that he could afford to sell sherry decanters at a remarkably low price because they were "total crap". It was no more than a self-deprecating quip from a respected leader, yet the throwaway remark resulted in the collapse of his major nationwide chain of jewellers.

Whether it is positive or negative, the critical point to recognise is: "You cannot <u>not</u> make an impression," by which I mean *everything* you do (or say), and *do not do (or say)*, will make some form of impression. I remember clearly the in-house stories that circulated about a new CEO who joined a major organisation I was working with some years ago. A charismatic leader, he made a point of always waiting to enter the elevator last, ushering others in first. On occasion, that meant the elevator filled to capacity before he could get in, and he would smile and wait for the next one. Despite the scale and complexity of his CEO role, it was his much admired 'elevator etiquette' that became the talk of the town. In contrast, many years later I happened to find myself sitting in the reception area of a different organisation, when their newly-appointed CEO entered the building. Looking suave and purposeful, he marched along with his small entourage past all present, to enter the elevator that took him straight up to the Executive floor - no interaction, no eye contact, no anything. I know that, over his term, he was admired for various reasons but also that he was seen by most as somewhat aloof and disconnected.

It seems Locard was right; the small 'exchanges' that were made at those elevators left traces that proved to be reliable evidence. Locard went on to explain that each 'trace' that is left *"is evidence that does not forget,"* and it is true that even the small 'leadership traces' we leave will be remembered for a long time. I hope the elevator stories made the point that it is in our smallest acts that we make our biggest impacts. Recognising that can place great strain on leaders who, consequently, are always under the spotlight. Yet, encouragingly, it means too that your opportunities to make a positive impact are endless.

"Of all the will toward the ideal in mankind only a small part can manifest itself in public action. All the rest of this force must be content with small and obscure deeds. The sum of these, however, is a thousand times stronger than the acts of those who receive wide public recognition." Albert Schweitzer, Noble Peace Prize winner

All this provides a great insight into successful leadership and relates well to the concept of what we call *'low-touch'* leadership. Many leaders do not have the capacity to spend hours in the presence of all their colleagues. They may not sit in the same office, building or even city, and they have only limited opportunity to socialise with their teams outside of work. Thus, the concept of *low-touch* refers to the fact that their interactions with colleagues are infrequent and brief, often just fleeting glances. However, far from this being a constraint, Locard teaches us that leaders can utilise every contact they have with colleagues, however brief, to make the right impact, to leave the right 'trace'. This explains why authenticity is so critical to leadership. Your actions have to be authentic because you simply can't keep faking it; it would be exhausting. Over time, the 'true you' will leak out, so get your leadership values right, and your many small actions will be authentic.

"Some people will like me and some won't. So I might as well be myself, and then at least I'll know that the people who like me, like me." Hugh Prather

Intent counts for more than technique

Given that the core skills and behaviours of leadership are clearly understood and should be easy to adopt, it is difficult to understand why people so commonly have a negative view of their leader. Why is it that so many leaders seem to struggle to deliver good leadership? I have discussed this with many practising leaders, and my conclusion on this conundrum is that people's views depend heavily, not upon the *skills* of their leader, but upon their *intent*. Our opinion has less to do with what a leader *does*: it is what they are *about* - it is who they *are*, that matters most.

This may appear to contradict previous comments about the primary importance of behaviours: it does not. The Arbinger Institute explain this well in their excellent book *Leadership & Self-Deception*. Their key message is that "skills are never *primary*." By this, they mean it is what you stand for, what your values are, and how you treat others, that impact most significantly upon those you lead. As Arbinger puts it: "People respond not primarily to what you do, but *how you're being*." For example, a person who is aloof, arrogant, and uses information as power will never be admired as a great communicator, even if they were a brilliant on-stage orator. They have great communication *skills*, but this makes little difference to how they are perceived. Similarly, for those leaders who at their core are deeply self-oriented and disloyal, their efforts to build a close relationship, to connect, empathise and inspire will all fail. These failures are not because their conference presentations were not well delivered, nor that their team social events weren't fun: they fail because the leaders in question simply miss the countless informal opportunities to communicate and build positive connections. When it comes to leadership, it is all about 'the small stuff'. That is why our *intent*, which influences our every subconscious action, counts for so much more than our *technique*.

This point takes us back to, and reinforces, Chapter 3 on Values-based leadership. Leaders must have the goodwill, humility and strength to be introspective. Taking a look at yourself in the mirror and assessing honestly how you come across to others, including seeking the views of others, may just be the most powerful leadership technique there is!

'Do what you love' or 'Love what you do'?

We have a generation entering the workplace who have been immersed throughout childhood with "If you can dream it, you can achieve it" messages. They have been told that the most important thing in life is to pursue their passion. "Follow your passion, not your pension" was the advice a business mentor once gave me. It is a wonderful heart-warming concept and something we all should reflect upon. For many of us, it will provide a helpful pointer in life. For a precious few, it will be the greatest piece of advice they ever received, as they head towards a mega-buck career as a rock star, pro-surfer, or even for those who have a passion for a more mainstream vocation. However, for others it can be unhelpful and potentially even a disaster. Let me explain why.

There is a phenomenal range of jobs and careers that offer fulfilling opportunities, decent rewards and daily enjoyment. Indeed, they make up most jobs that exist across the world. However, the interesting thing is that nobody would enter them driven by passion. One of my sons was looking at job opportunities, having just graduated, and encountered one from a major electrical utility company which posed the question: "Why are you passionate about a career with us?" Were they serious? Come on; a 21-year-old who is passionate about working for a utilities company! That's absurd. A far better question would be: "What do you think might be most interesting and exciting about a role with us?"

Rather than sticking solely to the: "Find a job that you love" mantra, we should also be encouraging people to: "Find a way to love the job you have." I truly believe this is achievable in any department, of any business, in any sector, anywhere! Indeed, I recall watching a presentation by US business guru Tom Peters who, in typically assertive fashion, berated his audience of leaders with the message that there are some people for whom you could "shovel s#!t", and yet still enjoy your job. On the contrary, he told the audience, there were other people who might have seemingly ideal jobs, yet they hate their work. I think most of us will quickly identify with Peters' blunt message.

Authenticity does not demand that we do only what we love and disregard the rest. Instead, it's about finding genuine reasons to embrace fully what we do. In any case, the job satisfaction options open to all of us are not bi-polar i.e. either we love our jobs or we hate them. Instead, our jobs are what we make of them, and different aspects of our jobs will fall somewhere between those two extremes. Think of your own career; I bet there were times your job description looked pretty unattractive, but actually you enjoyed the job, and *vice versa*. It is what we make of it and who we work for, that has the greatest influence on our job satisfaction.

We need more Amateurs

Lord's cricket ground in north London is the 'home' of English cricket and the famous Marylebone Cricket Club (MCC), and remains the guardian of the Laws of the game. Steeped in history, it hosted regular 'Gentlemen v Players' matches from 1806-1962. The Gentlemen team consisted of amateurs (paid only nominal expenses) and the Players team of professionals (paid a wage to play). The teams reflected Britain's social class divide; the Gentlemen were from the upper classes who didn't need to earn money from cricket. Remember, most cricket matches in that era took three days, which would not have been easy to fit in for a working man.

Over the 274 fixtures held, the Players won 125 games, versus the Gentlemen's 68; the rest were draws. It was a fascinating concept, which has no parallel in modern-day sport where professionalism has taken over, and it is very rare for amateurs to be able to compete.

Worse still, the word 'amateur' now carries with it some very negative connotations. If someone calls you a 'complete amateur', that is a big insult! Instead, we all aspire to be seen as a 'complete professional'. But, wait a minute, *amateur* derives from French, meaning *'lover of'*. Amateurs do what they do because they love it, and may even make considerable sacrifice to do it: 'professionals' do it because they get paid.

"People think I'm disciplined. It is not discipline, it is devotion. There is a great difference." Luciano Pavarotti

We see 'amateur' behaviour every day when people pursue their hobbies and interests. I doubt there has ever been a five-year-old child who first decides they'd love to be rich and then sets about becoming the best sportsperson, computer programmer, or whatever it is they enjoy doing, in order to earn that wealth. Instead, they love a particular sport or love computers and play and practise for hours. Any notion of financial reward comes much further down the line.

I have two friends who work in the medical profession. One is a specialist consultant, and whilst he is very committed to helping patients, he really does not enjoy the highly-bureaucratic working environment, nor the influence of a somewhat aloof senior consultant. In fact, he has recently retired, and sadly (because it was a job he loved) he is happy to be out of his profession. The other friend has cared for her special needs son for over 20 years and now works weekends as a cleaner at the local hospital. Yes, weekends and also Christmas day. I am sure the money helps a little. However, the point is she loves the job; she is an *amateur*! I bet she is brilliant at it, and I know she goes the extra mile for all the patients she comes across.

Few stories illustrate the impact of high work satisfaction like the Pike Place Fish stall in Seattle. Now world-renowned, thanks to the release of a video and book called *'FISH!'* in the 1990's, the business transformed itself from virtual bankruptcy in the mid-80's, to regain their strong financial success. The video and book reveal the amazing energy and fun the stall holders put into their work and how that spirit has delivered amazing success.

If working long unsociable hours in the cold, hurling wet fish around all day, can be fun, then we can *all* find a way to love *our* jobs! When we do, we'll be better than any professional.

Fake it til you Make it

"To be a great champion you must believe you are the best. If you're not, pretend you are." Muhammad Ali

Social psychologist Amy Cuddy's TED talk, *'Your body language shapes who you are'*, exploded onto the scene in 2012. At last count, it had over 40m views. In it, Cuddy presents the counter-intuitive advice that we should go beyond the old clichéd phrase: 'fake it til you make it', and strive to 'fake it til you become it'. For example, there are times when we might feel tired or apathetic, but if we are dealing with a customer or a colleague, we generally should present a more positive outlook. Similarly, whilst we may harbour some doubts about a colleague's capability, we should nonetheless try to encourage him with an optimistic view of how he can perform. In those examples, we are not being fake, we are consciously portraying a specific desired image.

A quick cautionary tale: we all know the wonderful story of the Wizard of Oz, and Dorothy's fury upon discovering the 'wonderful' wizard she had gone to such lengths to meet was in fact a meek and powerless old man, masquerading deceitfully behind a screen. Unable to contain herself, she declared: "I think you are a very bad man," to which the wizard replied: "Oh, no, my dear. I'm really a very good man, but I'm a very bad wizard, *must admit."* The wizard had found out the hard way that you can only fake it so far!

I am an advocate of Cuddy's advice, and her encouragement to 'fake it til you *become it*' is the key. If you do that, you *are* being authentic. What Cuddy is saying is that *what you do* (in her talk she focuses very much on your body language) does directly impact upon *who you are*. For example, we do a quick exercise on our courses, where we ask people to adopt an upright standing position, open their eyes just a little wider than normal, position their mouth just a little towards a smile, tilt their head just slightly upwards, and we then ask them to 'feel miserable'. Of course, it gets a laugh, and people quickly see the point. You cannot feel miserable in that posture, because our positive physiology impacts directly upon our psychology. If you are feeling miserable, it wouldn't be 'faking it' to adopt that physical position in order to boost your positivity. You are simply making a personal change, as a result of which you *are* becoming less miserable. It works, and it is authentic.

The example above is, I admit, relatively superficial, though it can have a big impact. The concept extends to any activity in life where we adopt the behaviours of the person we want to become. Just as 'you should dress for the job you want, not the job you've got'. That's not fake; it's ambition!

"Be yourself; everyone else is already taken." Oscar Wilde

In summary, leaders *do* need to perform/act. They need to project high energy levels when at times maybe they don't feel it. They need to get behind organisational initiatives when perhaps they don't fully agree with them. They may project a sense of trust and confidence in someone when in truth they harbour some doubts, but they do so to encourage, and to give someone a chance to prove themselves. Once you decide to be an inclusive and respectful leader, then behaving in accordance with that *is* authentic.

Impact on Trust

"Oh, what a tangled web we weave, when first we practise to deceive!" Sir Walter Scott, *Marmion*

Sir Walter Scott's poem *Marmion* makes the perils of not playing it straight very clear. Trust, supposedly, 'takes years to build, seconds to break, and forever to repair'. I'm not convinced about the first and last part of that. To the first part, some people do have the ability to build trust very quickly indeed; just think about how quickly con artists do it! Regarding the last part, some people discover that holding their hands up and admitting their mistakes with genuine contrition actually repairs trust very quickly. Take for example Bill Clinton's approval ratings, which at 73% reached the highest point of any President, immediately *after* his eventual admission of his affair and his public apology: *"I don't think there is a fancy way to say that I have sinned. It is important to me that everybody who has been hurt knows that the sorrow I feel is genuine."* Whether it was genuine or not, the fact is the polls at the time showed that the American people did accept his apology, and trust was restored instantly.

The middle part of the Trust statement, i.e. 'seconds to break', undoubtedly *is* true. Once we spot deceit, we are immediately alarmed. It hurts to be lied to or let down. Your view of that person crash lands, as you contemplate their lack of honourability and how low an opinion they must have had of you to treat you that way. Certainly, in the immediate aftermath, the situation appears unrecoverable.

Putting aside any potential that an apology might salvage the situation, the message is clear: "Don't put yourself in that tight spot in the first place!" As they say: "If you're honest, you don't need a memory." Life runs a heck of a lot smoother if you just resolve to be trustworthy.

"A team is not a group of people who work together. A team is a group of people who trust each other." (from *Together is Better* by Simon Sinek)

The Final Word: Authentic people don't bend with any breeze; they are more solid than that because they are comfortable in their own skins. That does not mean they consider themselves perfect - far from it. Rather, they recognise their weaknesses and work on them. It is this honesty that allows them to be at ease with themselves and to cope with the failures and criticism that inevitably come the way of ambitious people. As the Quaker William Penn put it: *"Buildings that lie exposed to the weather need a good foundation; you'll never make progress if you always stay sheltered."* Have the strength to be yourself.

Right level of Pressure

Inflating balloons requires you to get the level of pressure just right; too little, and the balloon is neither use nor ornament; too much, and the consequences are explosive!

We face precisely the same balancing act in a workplace. Too little pressure and people become complacent, listless and bored. Worse-still, surprisingly often 'the devil makes work for idle hands', when under-utilised people immerse themselves in unhelpful pursuits which act to your detriment.

Get it wrong in the opposite direction, and the pressure of work eventually becomes unacceptable or intolerable; people either walk-out or burn-out. Given all we know about rising stress levels, and the detrimental effect that is having upon people's physical and mental wellbeing, leaders have to remain attentive to maintaining the 'right' level of pressure for everyone.

Balancing Challenge and Support

How do you ensure people enjoy their work and feel supported, whilst at the same time challenging them to perform at their best? There is an inevitable tension between the two, however we should not see them as bi-polar points on a spectrum. Far from being mutually exclusive, they complement each other well, as shown by the *Support -v- Challenge* leadership matrix:

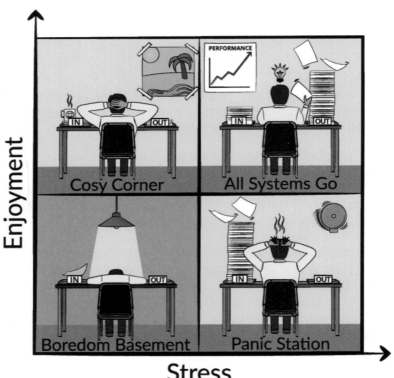

The 'y' axis refers to the type and amount of support that the leader provides for her colleagues. The support can come in many guises, such as formal training, opportunities to observe others, mentoring, coaching, rolling your sleeves up and helping, or simply by projecting an optimistic belief in colleagues. They are all essential leadership functions, and as the industrialist Charles M. Schwab put it: *"I have yet to find the man, however exalted*

his station, who did not do better work and put forth greater effort under a spirit of approval than under a spirit of criticism." But all the supportiveness in the world does not equate to great leadership. On its own, it results in little more than a cosy workplace, where people become complacent and develop a sense of entitlement. Think about those children we will all have observed who are nurtured to the point of being smothered. Rarely do they appreciate that support, and rarely do they excel.

The 'x' axis refers to the level and type of challenge that the leader sets her colleagues. This may be to come up with creative ideas and better processes, or it may be to raise service standards or productivity levels. Whatever it is, it is about the leader conveying her ambition to both 'do better stuff' and to 'do stuff better'. It is about everyone raising their game, which means going beyond their comfort zone. Having ambition and drive are essential leadership functions, and as the mighty All Blacks rugby team put it: *"If you're not growing anywhere, you're not going anywhere."* The best leaders are restless.

Yet, all the restlessness in the world does not equate to good leadership. On its own, it results in an exhausting workplace where the stress of ever-increasing challenges leads people to 'throw in the towel'. Daniel Goleman, in his work on Emotional Intelligence, identified six leadership styles, and researched the impact of each on performance. The worst performer was the *Pacesetter* leader, one who offers little support, yet demands high performance and wants it now! This type of leader pushes people into the Terror Zone and the Panic Station quadrant of models previously covered. The outcome is rarely favourable, and never sustainable.

True leadership only happens when there is an appropriate blend of 'support and encouragement' together with 'ambition and restlessness'. The two styles are ineffective or even damaging on their own, yet come together to form a powerful cocktail. We all appreciate being supported and find it exhilarating when we improve, and our confidence soars in the process. We admire and form affectionate bonds with those who help us achieve and pay them back with high commitment and performance. I have a business-owner client who says of all his employees: *"I want everyone who works here to get ahead"*, and I think that is a fantastic ethos from a business leader who aims genuinely to get the balance right.

Action Point:

Ask yourself the following questions: "Do you genuinely want everyone who works with you to get ahead?", "Where would your colleagues place you on the quadrant?" and "What could you do to improve your rating on both axes?"

"Few things help an individual more than to place responsibility upon them and to let them know that you trust them." Booker T. Washington

Get Out of your Comfort Zone

The concept of leaders stretching their people, and the benefits that that approach brings, is not new. Plato proclaimed this a long time ago, asserting: *"There is no learning without discomfort."* 'Discomfort' perhaps, but 'distress'? No! Plato simply meant that you have to get out of your comfort zone if you want to raise your game.

"The cave you fear holds the treasure you seek." Joseph Campbell

The *Learning Zone* may be scary but it is also vibrant, and with the right support excitement trumps discomfort. There is a balance to be struck between doing all we can to help people succeed, and helping others see that 'if you've never failed, you've never tried'.

We can illustrate this simply with the diagram opposite, showing three familiar zones:

If we fear all failure we'll never progress, and I endorse the acronym FAIL, standing for 'First Action In Learning'. So often it is from falling that we learn best how to get up.

If you train for a marathon, you fully expect long months of challenging training ahead. We know that the inevitable discomfort along the way is the only way we will get to enjoy the satisfaction of crossing the finish line. Goals like that are exciting, not distressing. However, if you overstretch into the 'Terror Zone, your training becomes grueling, you lose your flow, motivation dips, injuries occur, and your performance plummets. The same is true with any aspect of performance. Leaders need to get the balance right for each individual if they are to encourage them into the Learning Zone, but not beyond.

Action Points:

- Increase your focus on 'challenge' by making the question: *"How can we do this better?"* a part of your everyday conversation.

- Take an active interest in what people are doing to develop themselves, including in their personal lives - remember, all forms of development impact on all parts of our lives, which is why many forward-thinking companies actively encourage and sponsor non-work related learning.

- Make it a part of your routine to ask people: *"What have you learned this week?"* or *"What did you learn from that experience?"* Be ready to share your own answers too.

- Remember, most people respond better to manageable peaks and troughs in workload, rather than to a consistent unrelenting level, so vary the pace.

Don't Drift ... Set Timescales

Évariste Galois was born in France in 1811, and grew into an exceptional mathematician, with a particular love of algebra. Despite his intellect he had always struggled to articulate his algebraic theories. Academic papers he published from the age of just 17 were regularly criticised as 'obscure' and even 'incomprehensible'.

Aged just 20, having become heavily involved in the political scene, Évariste found himself challenged to a duel by an artillery officer. Precisely what triggered the duel is unclear, though evidence points to an exposed love affair with the officer's fiancée. A mathematician (who had brandished guns at political rallies but never used them in combat) had no chance against a trained military officer, and Évariste had no illusions about the fate that awaited him. Convinced of his impending death, he worked tirelessly through the night to put all of his algebraic theories down on paper, stopping only as the duel was about to commence. Just as Évariste had predicted, the officer's shooting skills were far superior, and he was shot in the stomach and died the following morning.

But he was right also about many of his mathematical theorems. The notes Évariste compiled in his final hours led posthumously to a revolution in complex algebra. After years of struggling to articulate his ideas, it was the awful deadline - or perhaps more literally 'dead line' - that spurred Évariste to produce overnight what he had failed to do over the preceding years.

People often wonder what it takes to come up with a big idea. Over many years, your brain will have made billions of observations, collected vast amounts of data and built an intricate web of connections. The reality is, *your* big idea is already inside you, sitting somewhere in your subconsciousness. What 'deadline' will it take to unlock the big breakthrough idea you hold within?

Évariste's story demonstrates the need for tension, pressure and an urgent deadline to force our ideas to emerge. Otherwise, the notion that we have an endless amount of time is debilitating. Our attention and thoughts become fractured and dispersed, and a lack of intensity makes it difficult to jolt our brain into gear, into that higher state of creativity. Just as Parkinson's Law states: "Work expands to fill the time allotted for its completion" we simply fail to be productive when there is no pressure to complete a task.

The working of the mind is like so much of human behaviour; we often don't do what we *intend* to do, yet we find ways to do the most incredible things when we *have* to. To unlock *your* big idea, figure out how to put your mind into a 'have-to' situation, instead of just a 'want-to' one. Although, do keep it short of a fatal duel, please!

Because setting deadlines is such an important component of what spurs us towards high performance, it is no surprise that in the field of goal setting, the 'T' of the SMART acronym stands for 'time'. Everybody becomes more focused when there is a time limit; even the most organised and disciplined person benefits from a sense of pressure. We suggest to leaders that their colleagues should, figuratively-speaking, sense your hand gently pushing their lower back. It won't topple anyone, yet it is enough encouragement to keep them moving forwards.

How is it that some people have that ability to get through tough times, and emerge stronger as a result? Like the puny boxer in our cartoon, some people just don't know when they're beaten. Let's be clear, they *do* experience the pain and hardships involved, but what differentiates them is how they cope and how they respond.

For these people, they live by the mantra: "Whatever doesn't kill you, only makes you stronger." As author J.K. Rowling put it: "Rock bottom became the solid foundation on which I rebuilt my life", and that is the point; resilient people face struggles but, like 'Robocop', they consistently demonstrate that knack of getting back up.

We can all learn strategies to be better at doing that.

"Winners are losers who got up and gave it one more try." Denni
DeYoung

Of all the challenges that face today's leaders, 'resilience' is on
that rears its head most frequently, and there are many reason
for that. Take working hours: even in my lifetime the meaning o
'working 9 to 5' has shifted from 'an admirably har
worker' (Dolly Parton even sang about it) to mean you are 'doin
the bare minimum'. Communications that took days or ever
weeks to send and be dealt with, because typing pools and posta
services were involved, now happen over a period of minutes o
even seconds. Workplaces are drowning in performance metrics
some places even measuring how frequently you use the
bathroom, and how long you take; make sure you eat your fibre
folks!

In an increasingly transparent world, pretty much everything we
do and say is recorded somehow, so we must be on our mettle a
all times. The relative calm of 'jobs for life' in which man
people could operate on 'autopilot' died long ago. In today'
world, we must navigate through far more turbulent careers, and
in many sectors working hours just seem to grow and grow. In
Japan, the term *karoshi* has emerged, meaning 'death b
overwork' – literally! Early litigation cases suggest employers face
serious consequences if they are deemed to have contributed
unreasonably to these sad events, so whether it's your mora
compass or the bottom line that spurs you to avoid these
situations, make sure the pressure people are under is reasonable
and sustainable.

"Some things are so serious you have to laugh at them." Niel
Bohr

As human beings, we are no different from those of recen
generations, so it is not surprising that the demands of today'
workplaces impose a huge strain on us. In 2016, the Health &
Safety Executive of Great Britain reported that 11.7 millior
working days were lost each year due to work-related stress
anxiety and depression. Incredibly, this figure accounts for 45% o
all working days lost due to the full spectrum of 'ill health'
Whilst it is difficult to know to what extent increasing workplace

demands have impacted upon the exponential rise in stress and other mental illness, it is hard to imagine they are disconnected. Whilst some improvements in working hours and working patterns are being reported, the workplace is getting no less demanding for the vast majority.

As leaders, we need both to develop as much resilience as we can for ourselves and also encourage the same in others. Let us be clear that 'resilience' refers to our ability to recover or to bounce back' from difficult times. It does not imply that resilient people never feel challenged, hurt or undermined by these difficult episodes. In the same way, courage is not the absence of fear, but the capacity to act despite our fears. A life without struggle and tough times is unrealistic, and anyone claiming to 'feel no pain' is faking it. Resilient people feel the strain just like everyone else, but they find a way to get through it.

The word 'resilience' derives from the Latin *'resili'*, meaning 'to spring back', just as a pole vaulter's pole endures huge stress in catapulting the vaulter over the bar, yet shows tremendous resilience' in springing back each time to its straight form. Occasionally, the pole snaps, and the vaulter crashes to the ground, which sadly mirrors life too, when things become too much for an individual to cope with. The analogy is a reminder of just how important it is to build and maintain our resilience. In this chapter we will look at ways we can do that.

Enjoy what you do ... the road to resilience

Steve Jobs wrote of his career: "I was lucky. I found what I loved to do early in life. Woz and I started Apple in my parent's garage when I was 20. We worked hard, and in 10 years Apple had grown from just the two of us into a $2 billion company. We had just released our finest creation - the Macintosh - and I had just turned 30. And then I got fired.

As Apple grew we hired someone who I thought was very talented to run the company with me, and for the first year or so things went well. But then our visions of the future began to diverge and eventually we had a falling out. When we did, our Board of Directors sided with him. So, I was out. And very publicly out ... it was devastating. I really didn't know what to do for a few months. But something slowly began to dawn on me - I still loved what I did.

It turned out that getting fired from Apple was the best thing that could have ever happened to me. During the next five years I started a company named NeXT, and another company named Pixar. Pixar went on to create the world's first computer animated feature film, Toy Story, and is now the most successful animation studio in the world. I returned to Apple, and the technology we developed at NeXT is at the heart of Apple's current renaissance.

I'm pretty sure none of this would have happened if I hadn't been fired from Apple. It was awful-tasting medicine, but I guess the patient needed it. I'm convinced that the only thing that kept me going was that I loved what I did. You've got to find what you love. Your work is going to fill a large part of your life, and the only way to be truly satisfied is to do what you believe is great work. And the only way to do great work is to love what you do. If you haven't found it yet, keep looking. Don't settle. As with all matters of the heart, you'll know when you find it."

By any measure Steve Jobs' career was stellar, and we all know the story of incredible passion that lay behind Apple's extraordinary success. It's an inspiring story, but it's only half the story of job satisfaction. As we discussed in Chapter 13 on Authenticity, seeking exclusively to 'do what you love' can lead many towards feelings of dissatisfaction, full of regret that ultimately, they failed to find that one elusive vocation they were born to do. The truth is, for most of us, there isn't that one magical pursuit, and our success and job satisfaction lies more in recognising that we can find and generate enormous satisfaction in every job. Of course you should seek a job that fits you well but it is as much about finding a way of enjoying the job you find. Rabbi Barnett Brickner provided the marital advice: *"Success in marriage does not come merely through finding the right mate* ut through being the right mate," and his words apply equally o the relationship we have with our work.

very job can offer meaning and pleasure, if you are prepared to ind it. Whether it is the pleasure of providing a product or ervice that others appreciate, enjoying the camaraderie mongst colleagues, solving technical challenges, 'sealing the leal' in a sales role etc., when you enjoy what you do, your esilience will soar. Being under pressure is far less of a burden vhen you are happy in your work. Help others realise this too, nd remember Pierre Casse's definition of leadership: "Leaders reate an environment where people can perform, grow and njoy." Ensure the environment you create allows colleagues to njoy their roles.

earn from the bad times

t is impossible *not* to learn from an experience. Everything that appens to us shapes us in some way. Exactly how, and to what xtent, is down to us; we own that bit 100%.

he remarkable fortitude of Austrian psychiatrist Viktor Frankl is vell chronicled, and he teaches us much about the power of the uman spirit in his best-selling book *Man's Search for Meaning*. espite spending almost three years in Nazi concentration camps, vhere his mother, father, brother and wife all perished, Frankl merged determined to overcome the horror and grief he had ndured. His experience of psychological healing became a ornerstone of his professional work. This centred upon the fact hat even in the most dreadful and dehumanising conditions, here is always meaning to life, always something or some hought that will bring us, however momentarily, to positivity. lis famous quotation: *"The last of the human freedoms: to hoose one's attitude in any given set of circumstances, to choose ne's own way,"* reflects his incredible fortitude.

he extent to which we are prepared to learn from adversity and evelop strategies to cope with those pressures will determine he cumulative effect of our struggles. Some people, sadly, follow a downwards spiral, where they gradually become ground down by the negativity of it all. Others, however, grow stronger learning each time to cope a little better with difficult situations and eventually acquiring a level of resilience that gets them beyond whatever life throws in their way.

"If you can keep your head when all about you are losing theirs, you'll be a Man my son!" from 'If' by Rudyard Kipling

Reflection Point: Consider a time when a negative experience left you feeling hurt or less able to cope. Take a big step back and think about what you learned from the experience and how might you apply that learning to develop your resilience. At the minimum, you should acknowledge that you *did* get through it! have no doubt though, that you will find other positives which serve to reinforce your confidence that you would cope again in a similar situation.

Watch out for burn-out

A coach of mine once challenged me with the comment: *"Long hours are the refuge of the mediocre."* I was, I admit, working extensive hours but most definitely hoped no one considered me 'mediocre'! Whilst it seemed a harsh statement, he did have a point, and importantly I knew his challenge was well-intended. The poster in my gym saying "Good things come to those who sweat" is a humorous nod to the inevitable link between success and hard graft. Yet, there has to be a limit, and here are a few reasons why I encourage you to keep a tab on your working hours:

- If it reaches the point that your work is all you have, you become one-dimensional. As Anna Quindlen put it: *"You cannot be first-rate at your work if your work is all you are."* Without other activities to balance the pressures of work and give you a broad whole-life perspective, you never have those much-needed moments of 'release', and you become narrower by the day.

- Everyone's productivity drops as fatigue eventually sets in, and at its worst we become so exhausted we don't even realise it. Just like a marathon runner who has started to 'hit the wall', despite ever-increasing effort and pain, we slow down, sometimes to a stop. Resilient people recognise that slippery slope and find ways to take a break and re-energise. Remember, even Olympic athletes take breaks from their training; they gear up for major tournaments but then let their bodies recuperate. We are no different at work; we need to take time to recuperate.

- As the quantity of our work rises, the inevitable counter-balance is the quality of our work declines; we should not kid ourselves otherwise. So, make sure you strike the right balance.

- The phrase *'stress carrier'* relates to people who, through their actions, lead others to become stressed, for example, leaders who have an obsessive attention to detail and work excessive hours. They send emails 24/7 and show little regard for people's workloads, putting others at risk of burn-out. That is bad news for them, and it is bad news for you too. It is your best people who eventually will decide enough is enough, and that heaps the pressure right back on you.

- Cultures where long working hours are the norm have become increasingly prevalent. Within such cultures, people's focus is upon 'presenteeism' i.e. the need to be seen to be present, rather than upon performance. That has to be ineffective, and at a human level it becomes impossible to lead a balanced lifestyle. The result is a recipe for stress, burn-out and damaged relationships in the areas of your life that become neglected. When those things happen, our resilience collapses.

"Half an hour's meditation each day is essential, except when you are busy. Then a full hour is needed." St Francis de Sales

Challenge your beliefs

"What is important is not what happens to us, but how we respond to what happens to us." Jean-Paul Sartre

As we go through life, most notably during our childhood years, we each develop our own unique set of beliefs. Those beliefs combine to provide a kind of 'moral code' that steers us through life's decisions, large and small, by informing us what is 'right' and what is 'wrong'. Some people believe that life plays out mostly in a competitive arena, and so act accordingly. Others view life in more collaborative terms, and believe life is best when 'everybody wins'. Some people embrace the YOLO (You Only Live Once) concept , and place a high priority on all aspects of fun and enjoyment; for them, 'live every day as though it was your last' would be their mantra. For others, that lifestyle seems frivolous and even irresponsible, because they believe that life centres around core responsibilities such as making the best of yourself or providing for your family. Only when those responsibilities have been attended to is there time for fun!

An example that will very directly affect our resilience is whether we have come to believe that 'life should be fair', or that 'life is not fair'. By the latter, I do not mean it as a gripe: I mean it in the sense of 'Tough luck, get over it'! I reached the belief very early on in my life that we are not all dealt equal cards i.e. life is *not* fair, and this has allowed me on most occasions to think more robustly about what I can do to resolve adverse situations. Whilst I accept and admire the spirit and aspiration of those who contest that 'life should be fair', I have seen too often how that can lead them into unproductive *'Why me?'* or *'Poor me!'* thinking. This example shows so clearly how core beliefs influence our experience of adversity and our ability to cope.

Carole Pemberton, in her book *Resilience, A practical guide for coaches*, explains how our reaction to adversity, and how badly it affects us, has more to do with our core beliefs than it does to the adversity itself. This makes sense; if you observe a group of people facing an adverse situation, each person's reaction will be unique. A boss who consistently fails to show his appreciation will most likely frustrate everyone in his team. For some, however, this would lead to mild irritation, whilst for others it could be utterly demoralising. The 'adversity' each experienced was identical, yet the impacts were vastly different. That is because, in this example, people have very different beliefs about acceptable leadership behaviour, about confidence in their own ability (which would drive a greater or lesser need for recognition), and about tolerating others' failings - in this case, the leader's.

Building resilience, therefore, demands we explore our own beliefs, and to check whether they help or hinder our ability to cope and bounce back. Unhelpful beliefs may involve fear of failure, perfectionism, unreasonable expectation of fairness, an excessive drive to be self-sufficient, unwillingness to tolerate competitive behaviours etc. Building your awareness of those beliefs enables you to recognise why and how adversity impacts you in the way it does, and helps you adapt in order to cope. We may still get hurt, but we are better able to control the impact it has upon us and better able to bounce back.

Keep a sense of perspective

"Almost always, your road to victory goes through a place called 'failure'." Bill Walsh

Resilient people retain their sense of perspective even when they are in the most challenging of situations. Our ability to view our lives in broad context and remain mindful of the many positive aspects, reduces the prospect of us magnifying the extent of our problems. Without that perspective, we will tend to exaggerate, at least in our own minds, the negative situations we encounter. For example, the presentation you made that was 'a bit flat' is reclassified in your mind as 'a total disaster'. Your boss, who is 'rather distant', becomes the boss who 'completely ignores me' etc. The ability to avoid these exaggerated negative interpretations is, thankfully, something that we all can learn to do. Take a toddler's behaviour for example. You can watch almost with amusement (unless you are the exhausted parent) how a very young child's emotions will swing from beaming delight to uncontrollable tears based on something as trivial as whether they are allowed to have a particular toy at that moment. What toddlers reveal is how little perspective they are able to access. It simply is beyond them to think: "That's not such a big deal, I can play with it later." or "No worries, I have other toys to play with." On the contrary, they are consumed by the emotional rollercoaster of life, devastated by every tiny collision.

Even into adolescence, applying perspective remains really tough. It is painful to see how some youngsters endure bullying as they go through their childhood years. Way too often the end result is a depth of sadness, and sometimes tragedy, that simply should not be. There are few youngsters who can access 'perspective' when they are isolated, humiliated and punched whenever it suits their bullying peers. Barack Obama made a point of trying to help youngsters in this situation, and his core message you may remember was: *"It gets better!"* It was a direct and admirable attempt to broaden their perspective, helping them to see that such bullying almost always recedes beyond late teens and almost always disappears beyond that. Instead of a despairing sense of 'this defines my life, and I can't cope', with greater perspective they can revise that to a more manageable level of sadness, and greater awareness that 'this is a passing phase of my life, and I can get through it'.

"However long the night, the dawn will break." African Proverb

Into adulthood, and as leaders, it is our responsibility to develop this perspective far more into our daily lives. As much as we may be driven towards high performance, and will plough enormous effort towards our ambitions, there comes a point when we have to see the wider perspective. Maintaining a sense of balance, where we remain equally connected to the wider aspects and positives in our lives, allows us to stand on much firmer footing, and not see every problem as a derailment. That firmer footing also allows us to see that we can lean on others too. Knowing that we can rely upon others to support and even protect us, provides a reassuring safety net for when the going really does get tough. Holding on to that perspective, and benefiting from that support, means we can get through pretty much anything.

"The hardest arithmetic to master is that which enables us to count our blessings." Eric Hoffer

Baz Luhrmann's 1999 hit *Everybody's Free to Wear Sunscreen* was based upon a Chicago Tribune article entitled: "Advice, like youth, is probably just wasted on the young." Amongst the lyrics was the advice: *"Don't worry about the future. The real troubles in your life are apt to be things that never crossed your worried mind."* It is a wise piece of advice which supports the role of perspective in helping us face the inevitable troubles that we *all* will face from time-to-time, whilst not draining ourselves by trying to predict them!

Accept responsibility

Doctor and psychiatrist Anthony Daniels served most of his career in prison medical facilities and wrote under the pen name Theodore Dalrymple about the psychological characteristics of the prisoners he encountered. One of his articles, *The Knife Went In,* discussed man's propensity either to take or to reject personal responsibility. In it, Dalrymple shares his common experience of serious offenders explaining away their violent actions as the fault of others, such as it was their victim's provocation, their parents' neglect, their peers' bad influence, the police's antagonism, or the system's failures that was to blame for their actions. In each case the language they used to describe their crime was 'passive', such as: "The wallet was clearly visible, so I was tempted." or "He insulted me, so I got angry." The words from two murderers he had attended happened to be identical, each declaring: "The knife went in." It is as though such people genuinely believe that an inanimate sharp object can summon the strength to thrust itself into a victim's body. *'The knife went in'* must surely be the ultimate example of absolving yourself of any responsibility.

Dalrymple's extreme example comes from the harsh side of life that his professional role occupies. However, think about how commonly we hear, and make, comments like: "Time just ran away" or "My previous meeting overran". They too are 'passive' statements, and they are dishonest. The fact is we *chose* not to keep track of time; we *chose* not to interject midway and remind the group of the schedule; we *chose* to stay beyond the scheduled time of our previous meeting. Stop blaming the world; *you chose* to be late.

Resist seeing yourself as a passenger in your life's journey: you are not. You are the driver, and your life is going exactly where you are steering it. *'If it's to be, it's up to me'* is a well-worn cliché, but that is precisely because it articulates perfectly the attitude of those we would all like to work with and for. It speaks succinctly about taking personal responsibility and ensures the end result is 'things get done'! Equally succinct is Margaret Wheatley's definition of a leader as: *"Anyone who wants to help"*, which refers to those people who step forward not backwards, look to help, contribute proactively, go the extra mile, and fix things when they are wrong. As leaders, we should recognise and reward all of our 'if it's to be, it's up to me' colleagues.

Be charismatic, seriously!

Why is this topic within a section on resilience? Well, because charisma and resilience are more closely linked than you might think.

The Oxford dictionary defines *charisma* as 'compelling attractiveness that can inspire devotion in others'. Charismatic people are often described as 'charming', 'having presence' or being able to 'light up a room'. As such, it is a concept that leaders should take seriously; those are useful traits to possess! That said, the whole concept of charisma is rather vague, and people can even be wary of it, viewing it as a superficial trait. Across different cultures, it can be seen as a sign of being rather oily, self-important, or even manipulative.

How then can we develop the 'positive charisma' that genuinely engages people? If you observe the common traits of people who demonstrate this type of charisma, you will invariably find what we call: "The *Four 'C's and One 'P'*," as illustrated opposite:

Charismatic people consistently demonstrate the following:

- They are *in control* of their lives and actions, and use whatever authority they have to take calm accountability for their responsibilities. They're a 'safe pair of hands': not a 'headless chicken'.

- They operate with the right level of **confidence**, which allows them to dance to the beat of their own drum and project their views in a clear and appropriately assertive way. At the same time, they avoid the trap of becoming over-confident or ignorant of others' views, and shifting dangerously from 'having an opinion' to 'being opinionated'.

- They are adept at creating a **connection** with people by showing genuine interest. Far from being 'silver-tongued', they are great listeners. Whether it is instinct or learned, they recognise that people feel connected to those who show respect by listening to them.

- They show *consideration* to those around them, recognising that they have a duty of care to those they influence. Leadership is a privilege, but more so it is a responsibility, and the best leaders are 'in it for others' at least as much as 'in it for themselves'.

- Finally, all of the Four C's are underpinned by *passion*. We are naturally drawn to people who exude enthusiasm; it is an admirable and infectious attitude, and it spreads quickly.

Notice in this model how there is no mention of white suits, slicked-back hair, gleaming Ferraris, or polished presenters with a fistful of clever comments and hilarious quips. Rather, charismatic people are just normal people who exhibit those five traits, which all contribute directly also to increased resilience. This is because they have the courage of their convictions, keep their heads up and stay close to others, and have the perspective that allows them to remain considerate of others' situations. For all those reasons, they maintain a high level of personal energy and dedication to forge ahead, regardless of the challenges they face.

Resilience and charisma act in perfect harmony. Follow the four 'C's and one 'P' and you will always bounce back!

"Tough times don't last: tough people do!" Anon

Section 5:
Summary

I have deliberately included many quotations and concepts which encapsulate the experience of wise deep-thinkers and, also, many accounts of extraordinary people who show the awesome heights to which the human spirit can soar. Such wealth of inspiration, overlaid with my own beliefs and experience of what works in practice, has formed the basis of my career over the past twenty years, and the basis of this book.

We are often caught up in the busy-ness of life, and so this final chapter simply presents some key points from the characters in the book. At those times when you have only a few moments to spare, this section offers some concise points to reflect upon and implement.

1. Leadership is Changing

Modern leadership has changed beyond recognition as the world has progressed through the Industrial and Information Revolutions.

Barely a few decades ago, leaders could rely upon a command and control approach to *Dominate* workforces, aka 'Push' style leadership. Today, at best this will result in grudging compliance.

The *Negotiation* style of leadership underpinned by Performance Management has done much to introduce a meritocracy in the workplace, although the systems struggle to capture all aspects of people's contribution and can be seen as cumbersome.

Today's *Inspirational* leaders form close bonds with their colleagues, recognising people as individuals and connecting with them at a Values level, to secure their full engagement.

The modern *Co-creative* leader adopts a 'Pull' style, consulting and empowering colleagues to ensure all their talents are recognised and utilised.

2. Creating a Great Workplace

The best leaders are visible and approachable, and role model the 'one mouth, two ears' mantra.

The end-goal for a leader is to create an environment where people can *perform* at their best, *develop* their capabilities, and *enjoy* their job.

Ensure colleagues understand how essential their contribution is. Chains break at their weakest link, and so everyone plays their part in success.

Look after others, and they will look after you. Demonstrate you care about your colleagues, and that will be reciprocated. People don't care how much you know, until they know how much you care!

Don't tolerate disruptive forces; address the issue head-on and with positive intent. If it cannot be resolved, part company without delay!

Vary your leadership style between *Front*, *Alongside* and *Behind* to suit each situation.

3. Values-based Leadership

Nothing defines and guides us more clearly than our personal values; the things we hold most dear. Our values form early in life and are deep within us, so take the time to consider what your core values are. From that awareness, living in a way that accords with and satisfies those values enriches our lives.

Leaders who are clear about their values are always recognised for their authenticity; people appreciate knowing what you stand for.

Be respectful when you discuss other people's values; they may well differ from yours but they are equally valid.

Connecting with colleagues and recognising their values is an exceptional way to build close relationships and deliver transformational leadership. Leaders who help colleagues to satisfy their values generate the highest levels of commitment.

4. Embracing Change

The first step in dealing with change is 'letting go', accepting that life moves on and we must leave some things behind.

An inevitable consequence of change is uncertainty. Learning to move forwards without all the answers is the only way to become change-oriented.

In a fast-changing world, standing still leaves us in an even more uncertain position.

Don't kid yourself you can predict the future. We all set out in unchartered waters and adjust our course as we navigate our way ahead. Mistakes are inevitable, but the biggest mistake is not setting sail.

Virtually all change is achieved through a process of many small improvements; don't rely upon 'lightbulb' moments.

5. Taking Risks

A life devoid of risk is inconceivable; we cannot avoid all risk and, ironically, if we tried we would risk even more. Nothing of note was achieved without *some* risk being taken.

When you shy away from taking a risk, ask yourself what is stopping you, and what is the worst that could happen. Being objective in this way helps us consider risks in perspective.

Be careful not to fall into the trap of 'analysis paralysis'. D assess risks with caution, bu acknowledge that there comes point when you have to 'let g and jump in'.

Challenge yourself and others t explore new territory. Expect few bumps, but new experience are where the fun lies.

Consider: "What's the worst that can happen?" Our fear c failure so often is exaggerated. Indeed, we *need* to fail at time: recognising the acronym FAIL stands for 'First Action I Learning'. None of us would ever had learned to walk withou that attitude. Go on, 'up' your failure rate!!

6. Positive Attitude

Don't waste your energy dwelling on what you *don't* have. Instead, capitalise on what you *do* have. The 'pint glass' of successful people is always 'half full'.

Work out what it is in life that contributes to your feelings of positivity and happiness, and resolve to do more of those things!

Recognise the positivity boost that 'helping others' is acknowledged to give; not only does philanthropy create positivity, it is a positivity that is proven to endure.

Develop the personality traits of 'agreeableness' and 'emotional stability' to reinforce the positivity that others see in you.

Positivity is a virtuous circle; the more you give out, the more you get back, so start that chain reaction now!

Being positive is also about being realistic; don't ignore risks and dangers, but don't exaggerate them either.

7. Continual Improvement

Leaders never settle; they always believe opportunities t improve are there to be had.

Embrace lifelong learning. The world is moving at an excitin pace, and advancements are taking place everywhere. Standin still is never an option; either you move forwards or you fa backwards. You decide!

When considering people's level of performance, recognise tha capability, confidence and commitment all play their part.

People grow most in environments where the commitment to learn and improve is encouraged and acknowledged. Never miss an opportunity to praise those who actively seek to raise the bar.

Create a culture where the fear of not trying trumps the fear of failure!

8. Coaching

The role of a coach is not to provide the answer: it is to *explore* the answer, and so the best coaches are skilled at asking good questions, and listening intently.

Be clear about when to coach i.e. helping others to find their own solutions, and when to mentor i.e. sharing your experience and dispensing advice. It may seem counter-intuitive but, on most occasions, people have the answers 'within them'; they just need help in bringing them out.

Be optimistic about people's potential; no one operates truly at their 'absolute best', and so showing an optimistic belief that others have the capacity to improve is the catalyst for all coaching.

Look out for others' limiting self-beliefs; most often, what holds people back lies firmly in their own minds!

Be focused in your coaching conversations. Whilst it generally is best to adopt an informal style, beneath the surface a good coach never loses sight of the purpose. Ensure you clarify what the coachee wants to achieve, and explore the tangible 'best steps' to get there.

9. Feedback

From the moment we are born, feedback becomes an essential part of every capability we develop. Thos who provide it simply demonstrate that they care.

Most of us progressively learn to avoid giving (and receiving) feedback, but the best leaders push back against that tendency, recognising that when we deny people feedback we also deny them the opportunity to improve. Feedback truly IS a gift!

Keep your feedback objective and specific. *"I noticed your voice tends to be monotone, and you rarely use pauses to allow people to reflect"* is so much more helpful than: *"Your presenting style needs improving."*

Make sure you also offer practical suggestions to improve. 'Feedforward' i.e. suggesting what someone *should* do, is a great technique to set people up for success.

Be even more generous with your praise; positive feedback lays the solid foundation upon which developmental feedback becomes valued and appreciated.

Finally, be a role model yourself by demonstrating a genuine desire to receive feedback on your own performance.

10. Handling Conflict

Recognise that conflict i.e. differing opinions, is both inevitable and essential. Without conflict, we would always plough the same furrow; we need the views of others to encourage new ways in ourselves.

Approach conflict with a constructive mindset; there is almost always some scope for agreement and advancement if people enter a genuine dialogue.

If you side step dialogue, and resort to authority, the best you can hope for is compliance. Commitment beats compliance hands-down.

Be flexible in your conflict approach. At times, you must fight your corner, but at other times it is appropriate to be far more open-minded and flexible.

If you do have to say: 'No', do so with empathy, and emphasise what you *can* do.

11. Allocating your Time

Stop saying: "I don't have the time." You have *all* the time there is; 168 hours per week. The only question is how you decide to utilise that time - what you prioritise.

Actions speak louder than words. "I was going to..." or "I meant to..." are meaningless statements. If you decide to do something, then *Just Do It!*

Beware the pitfalls of constantly reacting to everybody else's urgent demands. Some will be valid, but others are 'time stealers', and you have to learn to say 'No'.

Keep a check on your habits; they determine how we spend much of our time. Reappraise those habitual routines to ensure

12. Empathy

Make a habit of 'walking in others' shoes'. The empathy that follows will transform relationships and expand your perspective.

The abilities to empathise and to influence are inextricably linked. Without empathy, you cannot influence, and without influence you cannot lead.

Remember, 'taking your own shoes off' is the often-overlooked step to empathy. Suspend your judgement of others. Your experiences, views and beliefs are not theirs; theirs are valid too.

Finally, ask more open questions, and then 'Zip Up, and Listen Up'!

13. Authenticity

Remember, 'you cannot <u>not</u> make an impression'. Those everyday small actions we all take are what make the biggest impression, so make sure yours consistently send the messages you want to convey.

Your actions are important, but remember that your intentions invariably show through. Whether you drive people hard to ensure *you* are successful, or to ensure *everyone* is successful, know that your motive will be visible and you will be judged accordingly.

Authenticity is easiest when we enjoy what we do. Do your best to find something you enjoy and, equally, find a way to enjoy whatever you do.

Our physiology and psychology are intrinsically linked, so adopt the postures that stimulate the mindset you want. It's not fake: it works!

14. Create the right level of Pressure

Establishing a challenging workplace is stimulating, not terrifying. That said, ensure the level of support you provide at least matches the level of challenge you set.

It is only through being challenged that people can grow. Encourage colleagues out of their Comfort Zone, and into the Learning Zone. That is where performance and development take-off.

Set timescales. We all need a clear focus if we are to perform at our best.

Add 'restless' to your list of traits. It is not about being negative, rather it is about constantly scanning the horizon, pondering: "How can we do this even better?"

15. Resilience

Take time to reflect upon what you enjoy about your job, and your life. Keep those positives firmly in mind, and be appreciative of them. When difficult times arise, these positives help you keep events in perspective.

Develop a mindset that encourages you to learn from each challenge, and remain realistic that plenty of other tough times will follow, and confident that each time you will cope and you will emerge wiser and stronger as a result.

Find regular activities that keep you refreshed and, remember, as life's pressures increase so should your discipline to 'look after #1'!

Never let work be the only thing you have; we all need a life that is in balance.

Take full ownership of your life. Only when you see yourself in the driving seat will you take your life in the direction you want it to go.

Stop insisting 'life should be fair': it isn't! Just like in a card game, play the hand you've got to your best ability, and know that over time you'll be dealt good hands too.

Section 6:

The Future of Leadership

The Future of Leadership

In Section I of the book we outlined four key leadership themes that have emerged, notably since the beginning of the First Industrial Revolution. As the Fourth Industrial Revolution is now unfolding, it seems appropriate to reflect upon some of the bigger changes that are impacting our workplaces, virtually wherever we are in the world, and to consider how leadership must respond and, as a result, define the 'fifth' leadership theme.

The 'Fifth' Theme

Let us start with the inevitable acknowledgement that the future is unpredictable, and that humankind has a long-established track record of getting it wrong. Whether it's Lord Kelvin's 1895 prediction that: *"Heavier than air, flying machines are impossible"*; Grover Cleveland's 1905 assertion that: *"Sensible and responsible women do not want to vote"*; Ken Olsen's 1977 opinion that: *"There is no reason for any individual to have a computer in his home"* etc., we all know of hundreds of wildly-mistaken predictions.

"Prediction is very difficult, especially about the future." Niels Bohr

Much has been written over recent years on the subject of 'VUCA', an acronym originating in US military circles, which has resurfaced to describe our increasingly Volatile, Uncertain, Complex and Ambiguous world. Volatility refers to the scale and pace of change we are seeing; Uncertainty refers to the unpredictability of so much of that change; Complexity refers to the multi-faceted nature of the change, causing broad and diverse impacts; and Ambiguity refers to the lack of clarity and, therefore, potential for confusion around so much of the turbulence we encounter.

These factors all combine to make it ever more difficult to predict our future, yet to not even try to consider what is on the horizon and how we might adapt to succeed in that world seems myopic to say the least. Dwight Eisenhower put it simply: *"Plans are worthless; planning is everything."*

"No plan survives first contact with the enemy." Military maxim

Whilst any forecast or plan will inevitably be wrong to some extent, it must surely help to think ahead and consider what we should be preparing ourselves for. Plans must be fluid, but they all start out as 'Version 1'!

In this section I have picked out key factors that I predict will shape leadership of the future. In doing so, I acknowledge that future readers may well smile at how wildly mistaken my predictions were! Regardless, I do predict that these factors will combine to play a part in shaping the 'fifth' theme. Time will tell.

Artificial Intelligence: We are still human beings

What will be the role of Artificial Intelligence (AI) and emerging technologies such as robotics? AI has already proven it can outperform humans in many tasks, some of which you may consider to be 'functional'. For example, researchers at Stanford University have shown how AI systems can diagnose more accurately than teams of doctors whether skin cancer tumours are malignant or benign, although this type of performance is perhaps not overly-surprising given the power and precision of technology. However, other achievements have been decidedly more 'human', and the superior performance of AI systems is more (worryingly) impressive. For example, Facebook has trained chatbots to negotiate with humans, including subtle techniques such as feigning interest in objects 'they' didn't want, and *vice versa*. In an even more 'human' example, a Carnegie Mellon-designed AI system called *Libratus*, took on some of the world's best poker players in January 2017. It knew when to fold and even 'learned' when to bluff, and in three weeks it had won $2m from the pros.

There is no question that all these technologies will transform our worlds in ways that we are only beginning to imagine, however, to what extent they will transform the practice of leadership is far less clear. Take, for example, the explosion of knowledge that is available to us all and the pace with which that knowledge is updated or replaced; it is beyond even the best brains to absorb a fraction of it. Instead, the skill of maintaining a network of intellectual support will emerge as increasingly vital. That skill, of course, extends well beyond the 'mechanical' task of assembling a knowledge database. Not only do you need to know from *where* to get the information, you also need the collaborative relationships that mean *people are willing to provide it*, together with the *capabilities to filter* out from the plethora of information that which is unnecessary or inaccurate.

The Information Age will continue to provide incredible opportunities but, only through human interaction, can they be harnessed. Prof Meredith Belbin's book *Management Teams* published in 1981, introduced us to the concept of differing team roles; today there are nine identified. Within them lies the Resource Investigator role (RI's); the RI's are naturally outward looking and open-minded people whose enthusiasm and open approach enables them to form strong networks amongst a wide range of stakeholders. They may well not know the answer, but you can be sure they will find someone who does! The importance of 'RI' skills can only increase, exponentially, in future years. The difference between 'networking' and 'not working' is just one letter(!), and so leaders of the future will need to be master networkers!

How leadership itself might change is harder to foresee. We have referred for years to the 'Science' of Management and the 'Art' of Leadership, reflecting the more process-oriented world of management, aka 'doing things right', compared to leadership's emphasis on vision and personal interaction, aka 'doing the right things'. Geoff Colvin, in his book *Humans Are Underrated*, draws a clear distinction between the technical and left-brain skills that in previous decades were demanded for success, and today's emerging high-value skills that truly differentiate performance such as the ability to build trusting relationships, inspire and motivate others, and collaborate with others to solve complex problems. These supposedly 'emerging' competencies though are hardly new. For example, early Viking Laws implored members to 'find good battle comrades', 'agree on important points', 'don't promise what you can't keep', and 'consult all members of the group for advice'. On that last point, it seems the leadership theme of *Co-creation* has ancient, not modern, roots! These are all human traits, and they matter hugely because all peoples and cultures have a shared appreciation of them. Surveys from employment experts consistently point to 'soft skills' being the priority for employers of the future, all suggesting that 'soft kills are in reality the 'hard' skills, because they underpin all the ssential social interactions that fuel our businesses.

ike Colvin, try as I might, I just cannot foresee being 'led' by an I system. 'Informed' by them, yes, but to be motivated, ngaged, inspired, reassured, and energised by a computer is too uch for me to conceive. Whilst we can expect AI to bring us oth *smarter management* and *better informed leaders*, my oney is on people-centric leadership remaining every bit as key s it is today. I would go even further and predict that the human ouch will become *ever more* important, not least to ensure the erformance-enhancing technologies of the future are embraced nd harnessed to positive ends. Anthropologist Donald E. Brown ublished in 1991 a list of human traits and behaviours, called uman universals', which are consistently admired and valued by eople across even the most diverse cultures. They include actors such as empathy, generosity, humour, fairness and pride, nd collectively they bring us together (or force us apart, in their bsence). As a consequence, 'real people' will always be needed o fill the void left by these highly-productive systems and utomatons, and to interact with customers. It is in those ountless spaces that great leadership will differentiate erformance, perhaps even more so than it does today.

ge is just a number: The rise of Mentoring

he rapid emergence of new technologies, such as AI, will also romote a sharp increase in younger – probably *much* younger - aders who have the insights and technical skills to spearhead ose emerging industries. This trend will not just play out mongst our highest-tech businesses, although inevitably it will e most apparent there. More established businesses are already ecoming moulded on a system of meritocracy, and the guiding rinciple of 'best person for the job' will ensure that younger and ounger leaders will continue to emerge.

eyond the business world, the same inexorable trend will be in vidence. Much is written and admired about Canada's 'young' M, Justin Trudeau, voted in to lead his country aged just 43.

Yet, since that time, we have even younger national leader emerging, in Ireland (38), New Zealand (37), Qatar (37), Bhutan (37), San Marino (32), and now Austria (31). The latter, Sebastian Kurz, had been Foreign Secretary since the age of 27! How long before we have our first national leader in their 20's? (I am discounting North Korea's unelected Kim Jong-un who came to power aged 29.) Surely it is only time!

These changes are entirely consistent with the concept of lifelong learning, as discussed in *Section 7 - Continual Improvement*. Most notable is how typical 'learning journeys' have changed so radically in recent decades, to both 'decrease the disadvantage' and 'increase the advantage' of youth. Factors that help close the gap on older and more experienced colleagues include being less set in their ways, having less to 'unlearn', being less affected and troubled by 'knowledge redundancy', being more open minded to ideas and change, and being nimbler in accessing the plethora of knowledge available to us. It all leads to an encouraging picture for those who are young and ambitious, and they hold many of the keys to innovation.

All that said, experience will unquestionably remain hugely important. As Benjamin Franklin put it: *"An ounce of experience is worth a ton of theory."* Experience helps us to hone our skills, build the vital 'tacit' knowledge that so often underpins great leadership. *Tacit knowledge* embraces all the knowledge, skill and capabilities that people have, but are not easily expressed. Indeed, with tacit knowledge, people are often not aware of the knowledge they possess, or even how it can be valuable to others. The originator of the phrase, Michael Polanyi, described it thus: *"We know more than we can tell."* By way of practical example, I 'know' how to recognise my wife (she'll be pleased to hear that, after 32 years of marriage!), and I would recognise her instantly in a crowded room, but I would find it hard to tell you specifically how I can do that. The same is true of riding a bike, flying a kite, making a sale, or leading a group of people. 'Learning' such tacit knowledge generally requires extensive personal contact with people who have the appropriate knowledge and skills, and lots of opportunities to observe and absorb what are almost 'sub-conscious' capabilities. In short, the ey to acquiring tacit knowledge is experience.

s a consequence, the role of Mentoring will gather the same owerful momentum that Coaching has over recent decades. nthusiastic mentors have a huge role to play in helping those vith less experience to succeed in their leadership roles, ncluding the ability to connect with and gain the respect of older nd more experienced colleagues. Equally, the ability of mentors o balance capitalising on their experience, while avoiding stifling nnovation, will come to define the best mentoring relationships. xpect these skills to feature prominently in leadership evelopment initiatives of the future.

Good judgement comes from experience, and experience comes rom bad judgement." Barry Le Patner

Diversity: We've only just begun

have no doubt that the continued awareness of diversity, and he determination by most people to respect and support eople's individualism, is destined to feature ever more rominently in all of our lives. Leaders who embrace this, take a ead in promoting openness and tolerance, and make others feel nderstood, welcomed and supported, will almost inevitably rive positive outcomes.

have headed this section, '... We've only just begun', because I rant to emphasise that there's so much more for us to do in this rea, and those leaders who are non-judgemental on issues of iversity, and who display tolerance and support, will make a uge difference to our societies and be at a massive advantage. ur current approach to diversity seems to lean heavily upon xtending the 'categories' to which people may belong, such as ne LGBT acronym referring to sexual-orientation – an acronym vhich itself continues to be extended. However, I predict we will ome to see that our diversity efforts may be failing by that very nsistence to 'categorise' people, which in itself deprives people f their individual status. Our future leaders hold the key to orging a world, and workplaces, where diversity becomes an irrelevance and everyone can honestly feel: *'I'm not different I'm me'*, and they will gain hugely from doing so.

I think it is appropriate to at least acknowledge how much progress *has* been made on issues of diversity; there is a lot further to go, but the vast majority of us *have* come a long way. Forgive me for recounting a story from my early childhood, but it still amuses me to this day. I hope you will agree, not least because it was, I promise you, entirely innocent. It happened when I was around 7-8 years old, in the late 1960's, in a Primary School in Lancashire (NW England), when we were excited to hear that we had a visiting speaker - a Ugandan policeman! It was a unique scenario for the class; I don't ever recall we had had a visiting speaker, I had never spoken to a policeman, *and* this visitor quite possibly was the first black person most in the class had ever seen! We were totally transfixed by this solidly-built and jovial stranger, who told us warmly and enthusiastically about his family and his job. When he had finished speaking he asked whether anyone wanted to ask a question; you could hear a pin drop! After a long silence, a brave hand went up and we all sat in eager anticipation of what was about to be asked. The policeman responded with excitement, thanked the boy for putting up his hand, and reassuringly asked: "What would you like to know?", to which the boy responded unforgettably: *"What size shoes do you take?"* I never did find out why that was the information he wanted to know, but I have always held the view that he wanted to know something about the 'reality' of the man. To us, at that time, he was so incredibly different. We were all so impressed with this stranger and warmed to him instantly, but I think what we needed to know was that he was 'real'! We *have* come a long way!

Transparency: Keeping it real

Leaders are finding themselves under increasing scrutiny for most working hours of most days and sometimes well beyond. Conversations are routinely overheard or recorded, and for high profile leaders, the cameras flash relentlessly. Take, for example, CCTV - it is estimated that there are around 300 million cameras in operation globally, and no doubt that number will continue to grow. Indiscretions and misdemeanors, however minor, will continue to be exposed with ever-greater frequency, and levels of tolerance and forgiveness will continue to plummet. Leaders must find a way to demonstrate admirable ethics to cope with this microscopic 'transparency'.

The subject of 'ethics' is notoriously fraught; and well-meaning attempts to 'do the right thing' all-too-often fall on the challenge: "Who decides what the 'right thing' to do is?" Our increasingly complex and turbulent world thrusts ever-more ethical dilemmas in our direction, and whichever stance a leader takes, it will delight some and alienate others. To navigate through these ethical minefields, our leaders will need to exercise wise judgement in deciding the approach they should take on each occasion and, in doing so, progressively hone the following three skills and attributes:

. 'Honesty' is different from integrity; whilst the latter is about acting in accordance with your principles, the former is about having the conviction to say what you truly think. Let's say you hold the principle that it is good to be supportive and encouraging of others, and you find yourself asked by a bride on her 'big day' whether you like her dress. Let's assume you don't! Whilst your honesty would insist you said: "Not really!", your integrity (thankfully) would implore you to say: "It looks wonderful." The point of the example is to show how honesty and integrity are very different traits. In our business, we use the acronym PPOV to describe someone who is a 'Person with a Point Of View'; please note, it refers to people who have an opinion, not to those who are 'opinionated'. In all but extreme cases, honesty is universally-admired, and because you know precisely where they stand on an issue no time is wasted trying to 'read between the lines'. A willingness to express your opinion is a sure sign of confidence, courage and openness; all admirable traits. Additionally, PPOV's invariably value reciprocal behaviour from others and, in doing so, encourage open and honest debate, which allows fully engaged people to reach the best solutions.

2. 'Discretion', as they say, 'is the better part of valour', and leaders will need to exercise sound judgement to assess when there is no merit in adding their voice to a particular issue. As we discussed in *Section 10 – Handling Conflict*, the Thomas-Kilmann Instrument highlights the validity of the conflict strategy called 'Avoiding'. Sometimes the crusade *isn't yours*, and it doesn't pay to get involved. It may be something you can't influence, something about which you don't hold a particularly informed point of view, or even something that is too likely to lead to confrontation if you become involved. For a leader, on those occasions, to say: "I am aware people have very differing views on this issue, but I don't feel it would add value to join the debate" is a perfectly credible option in most cases. Avoiding a controversial issue, which a leader may well not have the power to influence, or may not be directly relevant to them, is often the most sensible thing to do. To state that clearly shows courage, not weakness.

3. The word 'Apology' has its roots in the Greek *apo-* (meaning "away from") and *logos* (meaning "speech, logic"), and referred to the offering of a defence or justification of an idea or belief. However, this original meaning has evolved, quite possibly triggered by Shakespeare himself, into today's accepted definition, which is an admission to someone you have acted incorrectly or inappropriately, and are sorry for the hurt or trouble you have caused. It seems, in my experience, that few leaders are able to demonstrate the simple capacity to say: "I messed up, I'm sorry, and I'm working hard to fix it." Instead, the issue is fudged with *passive* apologies that lack accountability, such as 'clearly, mistakes were made', and *conditional* apologies that ignore any wrongdoing and merely apologise for the impact, such as "I am sorry if you were offended." Both fall well-short of good leadership. The impact of a well-intended and honestly-delivered apology can be the smartest and most appealing action a leader can take. It is impossible to be flawless, so the ability and courage to offer a genuine apology when it is due must be in the armoury of our future leaders.

Personal Connections: It's good to talk

The most fundamental psychological need we all share is 'to be recognised', for people to acknowledge that we actually exist! That may sound bizarre, but think of any experience you have had of being deliberately ignored, and you will recognise how unpleasant that can be. If you ever experienced 'being sent to Coventry' (an English idiom, meaning to deliberately ostracise someone), often used by children to punish or bully others, you will know how severely damaging the impact can become.

It is precisely this innate need for recognition that accounts for the huge impact made by those leaders who are able and attentive to forming solid personal connections with their colleagues. Tim Smit, founder of the Eden Project in Cornwall, England has always promoted the importance of 'knowing your people', and is quoted: *"I say to people when they work here that they've got to say 'hello' to 20 people every day, read a book that they would never normally read, and then discuss it, cook a meal for all the people who make it worthwhile going to work, and make someone else's wishes come true."* Smit's career success, across many business ventures, offers strong validation of his 'get connected' philosophy, but our changing workplaces are making the landscape for doing this tougher, and leaders will need to adapt.

Even in the recent past, most workplaces comprised stable & co-located teams, which presented leaders with daily opportunities to build close and deep connections, provide support exactly when needed, and ensure there is appropriate individual challenge to stimulate high performance. The future, however, looks increasingly different, as the nature of our working lives continue to be revolutionised by factors such as the proliferation of 'hot-desking', the fusion of technology and mobility, remote working, working from home (WFH), and matrixed responsibilities. Whether it's the rising cost of office space, personal preferences to work flexibly, working across matrixed teams that require people to be in different places with different people at different times, or individual practicalities such as ever longer commutes, one thing is for sure, the days of routinely sitting alongside a close-knit bunch of colleagues are fast disappearing. Workplaces of the future will deny leaders those daily interactions, and new and smarter ways to connect will have to be found.

I refer to this emerging style as *Low-Touch* leadership. The phrase 'low-touch' refers to leaders having few, and often only fleeting, opportunities to interact with their colleagues. Their ability to make an impact, and make it quickly, will be instrumental to their success. These low-touch interactions compare closely to the supposed *Butterfly Effect*, which refers to "small causes having large effects", as in the flapping of a butterfly's wings setting off a chain reaction that results in a tornado in a distant place. The diagram below is not meant to induce paranoia: rather to raise your awareness that what you do and say gets noticed, it gets amplified, assumptions are made, meanings are inferred, and all of that gets passed on to others, and in our social-media driven worlds, that can be to *many* others! Of course, this is equally true for both positive and negative interactions, so those leaders who are diligent in optimising their 'fleeting' interactions will benefit hugely.

In many of the positive examples I have encountered this can be as simple as remembering people's names, where that is remotely reasonable, or basic things about them. You pay someone real respect when you remember their name, particularly if they wouldn't have expected you to. A specific example I recall well, related to a CEO of a global firm who was visiting one of the company's Regions, and the business update was, let's say, 'challenging'! Having delivered the candid message as encouragingly as possible he left the conference, but as he departed and said goodbye to the Regional President, he leant in, hand on shoulder, and said with an encouraging nod: "Keep the Faith." That interaction was recalled on so many occasions and shared widely; it was a fabulous example of low-touch leadership. Similarly, on a more routine basis, I have a colleague who is the master of the short, but high impact, telephone call. A typical call from him might go something like this:

"Hi Keith, hope all's well. Just a quickie as I'm nearly home; I was picking up on loads of positive comments from Smith & Co today about that project you did last week, and Gill particularly was raving about how dynamic the design was. I just wanted you to know, 'great job' as ever buddy. If it's OK with you I'm going to dash off, regards to the family and see you soon."

His calls are not quite as one-way as that, but you get the point, in under 1-minute you are left feeling fully reconnected.

Another factor contributing to the proliferation of low touch leadership is the increasing complexity of workstreams and therefore the number of people we typically interact with and need to influence, in the workplace. The formula shown below enables us to calculate the number of *relationships* (represented as 'R'), that exist amongst a group, based upon the *number* of people in the group (represented as 'N').

$$R = N \times (N-1)/2$$

For example, a group of 4 people involves 6 relationships; a group of 8 involves 28; and a group of 16 involves 120. In short, as the number of people involved in a team or a workstream increases, the number of relationships involved increases exponentially. Taking the example of a working group of 16, attending to 120 relationships is a mammoth task, and implies two things: leaders need to be smart enough to allow time for this to be done, and in pragmatic terms they have to develop relationships at lightning speed. It is a world for exemplary low touch leaders!

RIP Loyalty: Here today, gone tomorrow

There is another factor that will continue to place yet further importance on the ability to form connections. It is less a factor that leaders need to adapt to: it is one that they will need to *reverse*. It is the subject of 'loyalty'.

Whichever research you refer to, one thing is for sure, people are changing jobs increasingly frequently, whether by choice or necessity; in most cases it is probably both. Current research suggests the average person entering the workplace today will have had around 20 jobs by the time they retire. Many of those jobs will be 'zero-hour' contracts, offering flexibility perhaps (although this is more commonly a hollow justification), but certainly not reassurance. Indeed, we are seeing as a result a much greater incidence of people holding down more than one job, in an effort to shore up their low-income and uncertain lives. All this is a world away from the job-for-life careers of previous generations that bred loyalty. Admittedly, it would often be a very passive form of loyalty, at worst complacency. Yet people did have a strong sense of connection with their employer, they did build lifelong ties with colleagues, and they didn't spend their evenings on job search websites dreaming about how to move on. Today, companies neither offer nor, it would seem, *want* any sense of loyalty or longevity. In fairness, our turbulent world makes it very difficult for them to do so.

Future leaders will need to re-evaluate the desirability and do-ability of bringing loyalty back into the workplace. Loyalty is a sure sign of *intrinsic* motivation, i.e. an emphasis not solely upon *what* I get in return for working here, but also *why* I enjoy working here. It drives higher levels of commitment and reduces the costs of high staff turnover. People are people – we are human *beings*, not human *doings* - and leaders are failing in so many cases genuinely to engage, enthuse and enable others. I see it in so many places; employment for so many has become depressingly transactional. It is quite literally, at times, as if 'leadership is dead'.

There is hope, indeed huge hope, because that sad assessment offers the leaders of tomorrow the greatest of opportunities. Those leaders who find ways to reignite loyalty will create the most vibrant workplaces, where commitment will flourish. We all know that committed people outperform compliant people every day of the week, and organisations that create a culture of compliance can only hope that they don't encounter a competitor with a culture of commitment; it will be the shortest of battles!

In today's turbulent world, no organisation can offer a job-for-life, so how then can our leaders engender this loyalty? It comes all the way back to Pierre Casse's definition of leadership, where leaders must create an environment where people are encouraged to bring all their talents to work (they can 'perform'), they are given lots of opportunities to learn and develop (they can 'grow'), and the workplace has a positive and energetic vibe (they can 'enjoy'). It is not about creating a 'job-for-life', it is about ensuring it is a 'great job', and doing so will achieve at least five outcomes:

- People will stay longer, and be more committed whilst they are there.

- Motivation will be self-reinforcing, freeing you from the task of encouraging people daily – indeed, there will be days when *they* encourage *you*!

- Your staff will be your most effective PR agents with existing and prospective customers - there is nothing more appealing than engaged and upbeat staff.

- When people do leave, they will leave more considerately and amicably.

- Recruitment will be a breeze - your staff will take care of that themselves!

Notwithstanding the above points, we will continue to see vibrant and shifting workplaces that are more fluid than today's. Teams will need to be assembled, rather like 'task forces', to complete specific tasks, and a critical leadership skill will be picking a balanced team for the challenge at hand, and 'putting the correct team on the field'. As a consequence, leaders will need to be able to engage and enthuse people rapidly, accelerate the team development process, manage the expectations of those *not* selected and, at the appropriate point, be able to celebrate success and dissolve the team in a positive way.

Summary of emerging capabilities: Sharpen your saw

Our increasingly dynamic and uncertain world will only reinforce the importance of great leadership. Those leaders who truly put people first, and find a positive and inclusive path through our challenging worlds, will achieve great success and have an incredible impact on those fortunate enough to work alongside them.

Before leaving the book, take a moment to reflect on the skills, traits and practices summarised below, that future leaders will need to display. I have no doubt that to some extent my predictions will prove wrong. However, I remain confident that the list opposite will feature prominently in the toolkit of our future leaders.

'Future Ready' Checklist:

1. **Handle Ambiguity:** Be courageous in setting direction, but alert to changes on the horizon and decisive in changing course.

2. **Maintain 'Intelligence Networks':** Develop your *Resource Investigator* capabilities, and 'mingle like you're single'.

3. **Create synergies between Experience & Youth:** Give & receive mentoring, and share your 'tacit' knowledge.

4. **Embrace Inclusivity & Diversity:** Respect and welcome everybody, and make the 'labels' of today, irrelevant tomorrow.

5. **Display Honesty, Discretion and Apology:** Have the courage to speak your mind, and the judgement to know when.

6. **Forge Personal Connections:** Everybody has their personal story, and you should find the time to hear it.

7. **Excel at *Low-Touch* Leadership:** Make every moment count; small actions can have huge impacts.

8. **Restore Loyalty:** Make people feel they belong and have 'skin in the game'; you will win their commitment, and that will prove priceless.

9. **Role-model Emotional Intelligence:** Show your human qualities, such as empathy, generosity, humour, fairness and pride.

10. **Assemble Task Forces:** Bring people together rapidly, encouraging collaboration and, upon task completion, give due recognition before disbanding the team and moving on to new priorities.

I believe passionately that contentment, job-satisfaction and good-fellowship are of paramount importance in today's workplace, where stress and an ever-increasing drive for higher performance have become such common factors.

The road to becoming an admired leader is a long one, and it is as challenging as it is rewarding. Those who believe they innately are always right and who always act intuitively are likely to fall far short as leaders. Conversely, those who embrace the value of listening and learning will leap far ahead.

The much-admired Field Marshall William Slim considered great leadership to be an obligation, not an option, and always insisted: *"There is no such thing as a bad regiment, only a bad officer."* There were no hiding places for poor leaders under Slim's command, and it should be no different in today's workplaces.

I hope this book will serve you well as a leader, and that the huge impact you will have on others make it worth all the effort. This is not *The End*: it is just *The Start*.

Lead with Impact!!

References

(The) Arbinger Institute (2002) *Leadership and Self-Deception: Getting out of the Box*, San Francisco: Berrett-Koehler

Belbin, R.M. (2010) *Management Teams: Why they succeed or fail*, Abingdon, Routledge

Bridges W. (2005) *Managing Transitions: Making the Most of Change*, London: Nicholas Brealey Publishing

Bungay Stanier, M. (2016) *The Coaching Habit: Say Less, Ask More & Change the Way You Lead Forever*, Toronto: Box of Crayons Press

Byham, W. (1989, revised 1999) *ZAPP! The Lightening of Empowerment*, London: Random House

Colvin, G. (2015) *Humans are Underrated: What High Achievers Know That Brilliant Machines Never Will*, New York: Portfolio/Penguin

Covey, S. (2004) *The 7 Habits of Highly Effective People: Powerful Lessons in Personal Change*, London: Simon and Schuster.

Crofton, I. (2011) *Big Ideas In Brief: 200 world-changing concepts explained in an instant*, London: Quercus

Ehrenreich, B. (2010) *Smile or Die: How Positive Thinking Fooled America & The World*, London: Granta

Fisher, R. and Ury, W. (1987) *Getting to YES: Negotiating Agreement without Giving In*, London: Arrow

Frankl, V. (1946) *Man's Search for Meaning*, Boston: Beacon Press

Goleman, D. (2002) *The New Leaders: Transforming the Art of Leadership into the Science of Results*, London: Time Warner Books andy, C. (1998) *The Hungry Spirit: New Thinking for a New World*, London: Random House

oliday, R. (2016) *Ego is the Enemy: The Fight to Master Our reatest Opponent*, London: Profile

ughes, G. www.theodysseyexpedition.com

ohnson, S. Dr. (1998) *Who Moved My Cheese?*, London: Random ouse

ayira, L. (1967) *I Will Try*, New York: Bantam Books

err, J. (2013) *Legacy: What the All Blacks can teach us about he business of life*, London: Constable

lein, N. (1999) *No Logo: Taking Aim at the Brand Bullies*, anada: Knopf

emberton, C. (2015): *Resilience: A practical guide for coaches*, aidenhead, Open University Press

The) Red Bulletin (Aug 2017): *No Big Deal* (Article on free limber Alex Honnold)

chwab, K. (2016) *The Fourth Industrial Revolution: what it eans, how to respond*, World Economic Forum, Global Agenda

inek, S. (2016) *Together is Better*, UK: Penguin Random House

yed, M. (2015) Black Box Thinking: *Marginal Gains and the ecrets of High Performance*, London, John Murray (Publishers)

zatmari, B. (2016) *We are (all) the champions: The effect of tatus in the implementation of innovations.* Erasmus University otterdam, PhD paper

aleb, N. (2010) *The Black Swan: The Impact of the Highly mprobable*, London: Penguin Books

Wurman, R.S. (1991) *Information Anxiety*, London, Pan Books

Index

A

All Blacks, *Legacy* (James Kerr) - 33
Agreeableness - 85
Alive Time / Dead Time - 156
Amateurs, we need more - 183
Anaximander, Copernicus, Columbus - 109
Apology - 239
Aristotle, five ways to rule – 10
Artificial Intelligence - 232
Assumptions – 143
Authenticity, impact on trust - 186
(The) Black Swan (Nassim Nicholas Taleb) - 56

B

Brainstorming - 61
Buddha - 78
Burn-out – 203
Butterfly Effect - 241

C

Camel Fable - 139
Capability (Performance Model) - 96
Casse, Pierre - 28
Change Insights - 65
Charisma - 209
Coaching (definition) - 113
(The) Coaching Habit (Michael Bungay Stanier) - 176
Coaching Insights - 120
Coaching Language - 116
Comfort Zone - 193
Co-Creation, Leadership Theme – 19, 233
Commitment (Performance Model) - 100
Confidence (Performance Model) - 96
Continual Improvement – 91, 235
Criticism - 130
Crossing the Rubicon - 69

D

Descartes, René – 120
Discretion - 329

I

Ignoramus - 110
In Broken Images (Robert Graves) - 112
Inclusion, Leadership Theme – 19
Inertia - 154
Information Anxiety (Richard Saul Wurman) - 152
Innovation - 58
Inspiration, Leadership Theme – 16
Intent, counts for more than technique - 181
Intrinsic Motivation - 100

J

Jobs, Steve - 200
Johnson, Samuel - 103

K

Karoshi - 199
Kayira, Legson - 154
Kline, Naomi - 12
(The) Knife Went In (Theodore Dalrymple) - 208
Knowing - Enquiring spectrum - 111

L

Lawrence of Arabia - 37
Leadership & Self-Deception (Arbinger Institute) - 181
Learning Zone - 193
Lifelong Learning – 93
Limiting Self-belief - 97
Listen, and fall in love - 175
Locard's principle - 179
Longbow, practice regime - 159
Low-Touch Leadership - 241
Love what you do - 182
Loyalty - 243
Luddites - 53

S

Seligman, Martin - 80
Sharp, Issy - 32
Situational Leadership - 35
Slim, William - 248
Smit, Tim - 240
Socrates, Influencing (credibility, empathy, logic) - 174
Socrates, *Socratic method* – 173, 178
Strengths, focus on - 129
Support vs Challenge, leadership matrix - 191

T

Tacit Knowledge - 235
Time Management - 153
Timpson - 81
Thomas-Kilmann Instrument (TKI) - 145
Transactional, element of role - 161
Transparency - 237
Tuckman, Bruce - 140
Turn-Uppers - 159

U

Urgent vs Important (Stephen Covey) - 157
Utopia – 27

W

Wright Brothers – 59, 90
Who Moved My Cheese? (Spencer Johnson) – 54

V

Values-based Leadership – 46
V.U.C.A. - 231

Z

Zanardi, Alex - 77
Zapp! (William Byham) - 20